W9-AZX-079

TEACHERS
A Survival Guide for the Grown-up in the Classroom

TEACHERS

A Survival Guide for the Grown-up in the Classroom

by
Art Peterson

Illustrations: Josef Baar

Photographs and Graphics:
Frank and Judy Foreman

A PLUME BOOK

PLUME
Published by the Penguin Group
Penguin Books USA Inc., 375 Hudson Street, New York, New York 10014, U.S.A.
Penguin Books Ltd, 27 Wrights Lane, London W8 5TZ, England
Penguin Books Australia Ltd, Ringwood, Victoria, Australia
Penguin Books Canada Ltd, 2801 John Street, Markham, Ontario, Canada L3R 1B4
Penguin Books (N.Z.) Ltd, 182-190 Wairau Road, Auckland 10, New Zealand

Penguin Books Ltd, Registered Offices: Harmondsworth, Middlesex, England

For Norma

Acknowledgments

For their assistance, I should like to thank:

Claudia Reilly, my editor at New American Library, who conceived the idea for this book;

James Gray, Director of the Bay Area Writing Project, who led me to the right people;

My colleagues in the Bay Area Writing Project, Ed Allen, Linda Crittenden, Jean Dalton, Charles Evans, Gwen Fuller, Kent Gill, Milt Goldman, Dave Holden, Mary Hurdlow, Rollo Lewis, Jim and Virginia Pierce, Helen Salem, Lee Swenson, Mary Ann Smith, Bernie Tanner, Bob Tierney, Marshall Umpleby, Shelley Weintraub, and William Winston, who shared with me perceptive observations of school life;

Maurice Englander, former head of the English Department at Lowell High School, San Francisco, whose seminally irreverent attitude toward school matters has influenced the tone of this book;

The staff of the Folklore Archives, University of California, Berkeley, who were able to unearth some classic teacher jokes;

Vicki Chin, who skillfully typed the manuscript under conditions that must have violated some labor law or another;

And finally, my students at Lowell High School, who could have written this book themselves—IF THEY WOULD ONLY LEARN TO SPELL PROPERLY.

BOOKS ARE AVAILABLE AT QUANTITY DISCOUNTS WHEN USED
TO PROMOTE PRODUCTS OR SERVICES. FOR INFORMATION PLEASE
WRITE TO PREMIUM MARKETING DIVISION, PENGUIN BOOKS USA INC.,
375 HUDSON STREET, NEW YORK, NEW YORK 10014.

Copyright © 1985 by Arthur C. Peterson

All rights reserved

 REG. TRADEMARK—MARCA REGISTRADA

Designed by Julian Hamer

LIBRARY OF CONGRESS CATALOGING IN PUBLICATION DATA

Peterson, Art.
    Teachers, a survival guide for the grown-up in the classroom.

    1. Teachers—United States—Anecdotes, facetiae, satire, etc.   I. Title.
LB2832.2.P47   1985   371.1'00973   85-13665

First Printing, November, 1985
10
PRINTED IN THE UNITED STATES OF AMERICA

Contents

So You Want to Be a Teacher...

You were standing on the playground. Every kid in school had been picked for a team except you. Tears welled up in your eyes. Suddenly, you felt your teacher's hand on your shoulder. "Listen," she said, "when we go back inside, *you* can pass out the milk cartons." You looked at your teacher with awe and gratitude, and even though she was sixty-five years old and wore the same dress every day, you thought: I want to be like her when I grow up.

Or, perhaps your desire to teach began when you first noticed the amount of power your teacher wielded in the classroom: How nice it would be to control the lives of others, to decide when people might have a drink of water or a bowel movement.

Then again, you might have decided to become a teacher because you have a deep love for learning, children, and the smell of fresh ditto papers. Whatever the reason, you think you want to be a teacher. But are you truly suited for the profession? Do you have the bladder of a horse? Are you eager to take a pov-erty vow without the luxury of living rent-free in a convent? How many times a day can you bear to look inside people's mouths for bubble gum? In other words: Are you teacher material?

Are You Teacher Material?

Do you want to educate young people?
So you can make the world a better place?
And still get off work by 3:30?

Do you like school?
And would you enjoy working with kids?
Who don't?

Are you a serious scholar?
Who likes teaching?
And monitoring cafeterias?

Do you enjoy meeting new people?
Who remind you of yourself?
When you were an obnoxious kid?

Are you a tactful person?

Who can talk to parents about their children's problems?

When the children's problems are their parents?

Do you want to have a two-month summer vacation?

So you can do fun things?

Like teach summer school?

Would you like to work with kids?

Who enjoy learning?

As long as what they're learning about is Michael Jackson?

Do you like to eat?

Exotic foods?

Such as Bar-B-Que Meat Loaf Squares?

You can answer "Yes" to these questions? Maybe you *are* teacher material. If you're still uncertain, the following test should help you.

★★★

The Official Teacher Aptitude Test

★★★

Teaching is a job everyone thinks he can do.

But only the Official Teacher Aptitude Test will let you know if you have the talent and temperament to serve as the professional descendant of Socrates, Alfred North Whitehead, and Mr. Peepers. So get out your #2 pencil, and circle the answers you think are correct:

1. The morning paper headlines "SECOND COMING EXPECTED TODAY."
You should:
   a. call in sick.
   b. excuse students from class, but only with a verified note from their parents.
   c. have students outline the news story and present it during current events period.

2. "If you do that one more time..."
The teacherly way to finish this sentence is:
   a. "...I'll join you."
   b. "...you might get it right."
   c. "...I'll send you to (the girls' dean, Des Moines, Purgatory"—whichever seems most intimidating at the moment).

3. **Looking at the above configuration, your first inclination is to:**
   a. get your eyes checked.
   b. put it under a microscope.
   c. tell it to form a line of twos and stop the visiting.

4. **You have just finished a year in which your creativity and re-sourcefulness have brought extraordinary benefits to the institution for which you work. The anticipated reward for this accomplishment is:**
   a. an office on the fortieth floor with a view of the Manhattan skyline.
   b. a fully paid month-long junket to a secluded spa where you can wallow in vintage wine, gourmet food, and exotic sex.
   c. a nice letter in your personnel file . . . maybe.

5. **A teenage driver cuts in front of you, almost causing a rear-end collision. Your teacherly inclination would be:**
   a. to call the police.
   b. to shrug, and mumble, "Kids these days . . ."
   c. to notify the dean that Richie Saltrap has boosted the driver's training car again.

6. **You are enrolled in education school and your professor says, "Recent research shows that the more time a child spends practicing a school task, the more likely she is to learn it." A good question for the professor might be:**
   a. Isn't that common sense?
   b. Does that mean that the more busy work a kid is given, the busier he'll learn to be?
   c. May I have my credential now?

7. **Which of the following student questions qualifies as totally inappropriate in a classroom:**
   a. Do we have to use ink?
   b. Can we turn this in tomorrow?
   c. Why are we doing this stuff anyway?

8. **Which social reform is the *least* realistic?**
   a. Eliminating world hunger.
   b. Achieving permanent peace.
   c. Changing the janitor's schedule so he doesn't sweep your classroom during your ten o'clock reading group.

9. **Simulation test**
   - Rent a room about the size of an average classroom.
   - Pile into it as many people under eighteen years of age as can uncomfortably fit.
   - Then pour in thirteen more.
   - Rent a public-address system and hire an actor with a voice like Jerry Lewis's to announce at one-minute intervals: "Robert Hooligan is needed in the main office."
   - Hire eighty-seven monitors to enter the room at half-minute intervals with emergency notices such as: "The bus that usually leaves at 2:48 will leave at 2:50 today."
   - Position a ghetto blaster tuned to full volume outside a window.
   - Make sure the classroom clock is stuck at the time for dismissal.
   - Hire a girl to drop the contents of her purse on the floor each time things begin to calm down.
   - While all this is going on, deliver a lecture on osmosis.

NOW ANSWER THIS TRUE-FALSE QUESTION:

I, _____, **being of sound mind and body, want to be a teacher.**

T   F

Answer Key

1. **C.** This was a thought question. If you missed it, YOU DID NOT HAVE YOUR THINKING CAP ON.
2. **C** is the correct answer, though A and B are often used by teachers who change jobs frequently.
3. **C** is the correct answer, though some permissive teachers may allow quiet talking.
4. **C.** Any other suggests you are taking this merit-pay talk far too seriously.
5. **C** is the correct answer, of course.
6. **C.** Do not forget that the object of education school is to get through it.
7. **C** would be the correct answer. If you missed it, we suggest you get

a Ph.D. and teach graduate school, where "Why are we doing this stuff?" would be an appropriate question that nobody ever asks.

8. C is the correct answer. Do not even breathe loud about such a change unless you want to be labeled a rabble-rouser, a Leninist, or a member of the AFT.

9. If you answered "True" after taking this simulation test, we do not want you, but we will take you.

Eighteen Reasons to Be a Teacher

So you still want to be a teacher. That's OK, but you had better be ready for the Question. The Question is, "ARE YOU CRAZY?" Of course, the most precise, eloquent, and expeditious answer to the Question is "Yes," but, in case you feel some masochistic need to elaborate on your compulsion, here are eighteen perfectly logical reasons to become a teacher that any psychiatrist can understand. You should become a teacher if:

1. You want to get home before the rush hour starts, even if you have to drive a 1968 Dodge Dart to do it.

2. You want your summers free so you can scrape together a living by driving a cab, tending bar, and selling Fuller brushes.

3. You are a natural actor, unfazed by an audience that eats Fritos, applies nail polish, and cracks Double Bubble during your performance.

4. You want to keep learning, especially about the chief exports of Liberia.

5. You are never wrong and are always the first to admit it.

6. You want to prove to your mother that even if you can't pass geometry, at least you can teach it.

7. You want to impress your friends—particularly those under age eleven.

8. You enjoy tinkering with overhead projectors in your spare time.

9. Your favorite movie is *DNA and You*.

10. You want to be able to write any trip farther away than the Laundromat off your income tax.

11. You love moron jokes.

12. You have neat handwriting.

13. You particularly love moron jokes.

14. You want to be called "Mr." or "Ms." even if your starting pay is only $12,500 a year.

15. Your idea of a good summer beach read is Bragdon and McKutchin's *History of a Free People*.

16. You love kids. Or perhaps, more precisely—you hate adults.

17. You are a whiz at making stuff out of Popsicle sticks and egg cartons.

18. You *really* love moron jokes.

Why I Became a Teacher: Five True and Moving Confessions

"As long as I can remember, I have been fascinated by questions such as, 'What nineteenth-century battle was lost when a commanding general was incapacitated by diarrhea?'"

—T. Rivial Pursuit

"I like the food in the cafeteria."

—Vera Hungry

Why I Became a Teacher: Five True and Moving Confessions

"It was 1972. We were rejecting money, power, status, and parents. 'Folks,' I said, 'I've taken a job teaching seventh-grade social studies.' Well, I might as well have said I was joining the Weather Underground. My mother cried; my father shook: 'Is that what we sent you to college for? To become a schoolteacher?' Sure, since that day, I've had my doubts, but I still enjoy watching everyone squirm at family gatherings when I interrupt talk about how rich my cousin the brain surgeon is to tell everybody the details of last week's field trip to the Calumet Paper Box Factory."

—Rubin Marcuse

Why I Became a Teacher: Five True and Moving Confessions

"I used to sell baby clothes for Infant Wear International. It was a horrible job—I had to travel all over the Southwest and never got to be home. Well, one night I ran into a teacher in a bar who kept talking about how he was 'a salesman for ideas.' Anyhow, I was a little drunk, and I figured if I could sell baby clothes, I could sell anything. So I decided to become 'a salesman for ideas.' I'll tell you—the hours are good and I like being home nights, but I sure am glad I'm not working on commission."

—*Willa Loman*

Why I Became a Teacher:
Five True and Moving Confessions

"Well, the truth is, I started out teaching with the idea that it was something to do until I got married. That was ten years ago. You know any men over the age of seventeen?"

—*Miss (Not Ms.) Hope Wedbell*

★★

Surviving Teacher Education

★★

As an education major, under stand you may fall into a common pattern. Your college Education Department may be an academic Bermuda Triangle where potential teaching candidates mysteriously disappear, only to show up weeks later dispensing piña coladas at some fern bar. However, unlike their bartending colleagues, these ex— teaching candidates have not flunked out of school. Education students drop out not because of the intellectual rigor of their professional preparation, but because of its absence.

However, with the proper mindset, most anyone who wants to be a teacher can get through the required education courses. Like a winter in Siberia or a prostate exam, education school is not so bad if you know what to expect. Here are some pointers.

1. *Don't try to buck the system.* The education school is a monopoly. To complain to the dean about too many Mickey Mouse courses will do as much good as complaining to the president of AT&T about too few Mickey Mouse phones.

2. *Understand the hidden agenda.* A principal purpose of education school is to burden you with a dose of healthy guilt that will motivate you to try to succeed against ridiculous odds for the next thirty years or so. You will find that education professors do not approve of lectures, exams, grades, homework, "tracking," memorization,

textbooks, required curriculum, proper footnotes, or much else that goes on in schools, with the possible exception of recess. However, as you cannot work one day as a teacher without engaging in these odious practices, you must either learn to live with the guilt this rigidity produces OR entertain the possibility that your professor is wrong.

A little test will help you measure your instructor's dedication to educational right-think. Does she herself insist on class attendance, legible handwriting, or other "lock-step" requirements that could very well dim your inherent interest in learning about creative bulletin-board construction or whatever other important subject is at hand? If so, there is no reason to pay her special heed. She is just like the rest of us: making the world safe for hypocrisy.

3. *Master special techniques to survive the educational theory courses.* The real killer courses in education school are not the ones in which you learn to do wonderful things with egg cartons and papier-mâché. Properly understood, these courses can be a lot like a session in summer camp. It's the course "Philosophical Foundations of American Public Education" that can be as dreary as a New Age encounter group without the sexual possibilities. But, like it or not, as a student in the education department you are going to confront a course with a description like:

Survey of theoretical and clinical

approaches to the facilitation of teaching techniques with emphasis on cross-cultural learning, communication dynamics, multiple assessment procedures and differential diagnostic tools. Particular attention will be given to analysis of societal norms as they affect the education of the deviant learner.

Do you think I made this up?

When you are required to take a course like this, keep your mouth shut and assume the demeanor of a diligent note-taker. Make grocery lists, catalogue the sexual positions of the *Kama Sutra*, write 5,000 times, "I refuse to go crazy." Then, when you are asked to write a final examination essay, do not bother much about answering the question you have been asked, but instead get these sentences—neatly written—into your answer:

a. Our schools reward only left-brain lateral thinking.

b. In education, androgyny is the way to go.

c. The best teachers are in touch with their feelings.

d. Teachers need to understand that the legitimacy of the dialect of the white middle class is just another white-middle-class thing.

If you manage to squeeze all four of these statements into your final exam, you may be confident of a high grade.

Grade School or High School?

Unlike doctors and lawyers, teachers must specialize *before* their training begins. To know that you want to be a teacher is not good enough. At the tender age of eighteen, you must decide whether you want to be a grade school or a high school teacher. And, as with most decisions made at the age of eighteen, the odds are that left to your own choice, you will make the *wrong* decision.

To make certain that you end up in the environment where you will survive (if not thrive), you should take the following quiz.

And remember: YOU ARE THE GRADE YOU TEACH.

The Teacher Specialty Quiz

Directions: Circle A or B.

1. If I were forced to enter a boys' bathroom in order to break up a fight, I would rather see:

a. small genitalia.

b. large genitalia.

2. Regarding my social life, I would rather spend my evenings:

a. Grading two hundred papers —all on different subjects.

b. Grading two hundred papers —all on the same subject.

3. If one of my students had an "accident," I would:
   a. clean it up.
   b. throw up.

4. When students stick out their tongues, they are:
   a. being fresh.
   b. French kissing.

5. True or false: Someday, I will have saved enough money to buy a house.
   a. False.
   b. False.

ANSWER KEY: If you circled a majority of A's, get ready for a lifetime of fun and games in grade school. Develop a thick skin that will serve you well after you have heard your forty-third book report on Judy Blume's *Tales of a Fourth Grade Nothing*.

If you circled a majority of B's, get ready for a lifetime of fun and games in high school. Develop a thick skin that will serve you well after you have heard your forty-third book report on Blanche Knott's *Truly Tasteless Jokes*.

● 2 ●
The First-Year Teacher's Survival Manual; or, Don't Smile until Christmas

As a first-year teacher, your primary task will be to forget everything you were taught by professors in education school, and start learning everything taught by drill sergeants in boot camp. You are a soldier now, subject to airplane attacks (notebook paper can be quite sharp when folded to resemble a B52 bomber), bouts of rare diseases (if the students don't give you dysentery, the cafeteria food will), and peculiar forms of torture (there would have been no need to destroy Hiroshima if someone had flown overseas thirty-two second-graders armed with a variety of half-remembered "Knock-Knock" jokes). So memorize the rules below and you will be as prepared for battle as any neophyte soldier sent into enemy territory without a gun:

How to Survive the First Day: Five Rules

Rule #1: Don't smile. As far as your students are concerned, a smiling teacher is a vulnerable teacher, and a vulnerable teacher is a dead duck. So resist those welcoming grins your students force on you the first day of class: You are being tested, not greeted.

Rule #2: Don't blink. A blink lasts a fraction of a second. Not much time from an adult's perspective, but an eternity to a child about to let out a nice, loud fart just as you introduce yourself. Even fairly young children have heard that all human beings blink. You, therefore, must be an extra-terrestrial. Not a bad first-day image.

Rule #3: Memorize your students' names before you meet them. Plead with your school's secretary until you receive the file of each student who is to be a member of your class. These files usually include hopelessly out-of-date photographs of students. So ignore hairstyles, runny noses, and zits. Focus on the eyes. First-year teachers who are able to greet students by name at the start of the school year are thought to be witches and warlocks by grade-school-age children. (Incidentally, you can reinforce this impression by learning the exact moments when the bells ring and then saying "ABRACADABRA" immediately prior to them.) As for older students, even the most hardened eighteen-year-old will be thrown off guard if you turn to him on the first day of class and say, "Why, hello there, John Smith. How are your parents, Ralph and Mary? Have you seen your father much since the divorce two years ago?"

Rule #4: Refuse all requests for personal information. Many first-year teachers spend the evening before school starts rehearsing lengthy introductory speeches. Toss into your garbage any piece of paper that contains more than "Hello, my name is ————, and I'm your new teacher." As far as students are concerned, they are detectives and you are the mystery they must solve. They will remain interested in what you have to say as long as you remain inscrutable. Give away too much too soon and no one will be paying attention in October when you're trying to teach about prepositions. Keep as many secrets as you can. Above all, do not reveal your first name. (There is a direct correlation between the amount of noise in a classroom and the number of students in that classroom who know the teacher's first name.)

Rule #5: Leave your bulletin boards blank. Attractively decorated bulletin boards signal to students that you care about them and are eager to have them in your room. Well, maybe you *do* care about them, and *are* eager to have them in your room, but why should you let them see your trump card? (*See Rule #4.*) If policy at your school requires that you decorate bulletin boards, consider doing what one battle-seasoned teacher did: Place an elaborate, construction-paper headline across the top of your bulletin board that reads F PAPERS. Everyone, students and administrators included, will hope that ominous board remains barren.

The First-Year Teacher's Guide to Competency Tests

You think, because you have eighteen years of schooling, the character of Mother Theresa, and an uncle on the School Board, that you are going to get a job teaching. You're wrong. You must also be competent. Many states now give Teacher Competency Tests. To prove your competency, you will need to answer questions such as, "What is the numerical value of pi?" And we are not talking here about Mom's apple. To help you prepare for such tests, take the following quiz.

Are You Competent?: A Quiz

MATH

1. If the three administrators evaluating your performance have a combined I.Q. of 210 and a total of 4.2 years classroom teaching experience, what will be their average score on the Hirshfield Insecurity Scale on the day they summon you for an evaluation conference?

2. The National Education Association has found that the average length of service of teachers, many of whom are dissatisfied with their jobs, has dropped from twenty years to fourteen years over the past two decades. At this rate of decline, how many years will it take before the average teacher quits a year before he starts?

READING COMPREHENSION

3. *The history of American student life is not one of revolutionary fervor; it's one of nice, little, rich, white ladies and gentlemen getting C-plus educations to go out and become C-plus consumers.*

　　　　　　　—Abbie Hoffman

From this selection, we may conclude:
   a. Abbie Hoffman is a hard grader.
   b. Nice, *big*, rich, white ladies and gentlemen are better teachers than nice, *little*, rich, white ladies and gentlemen.
   c. There is a need for better consumer education in our schools.

LOGIC

4. Japanese students spend 240 days a year in school; eighty-five percent of this time is spent on instruction. American students spend 180 days a year in school, twenty-five percent of it on instruction. Therefore, it follows that:
   a. Education has nothing to do with winning world wars.
   b. The number of hours Japanese students spend studying is roughly equivalent to the number of hours American students spend watching MTV.
   c. We will soon be able to catch up to the Japanese with a crash program that increases the number of school days to 410 days a year.

EDUCATIONAL THEORY

5. If your principal tells you that "a gross assessment of the average mean score in your classroom indicates that your students have begun to plateau out," you should answer:

    a. "If you can't say anything nice, don't say anything at all."

    b. "My horoscope said this was going to happen."

    c. "So that's why they forget to bring their milk money."

6. If adapting the principles of Bloom's Taxonomy to a particular text or curriculum is known as "Blooming it" (no kidding!), returning to the educational principles of John Dewey would be:

    a. Deweying it.

    b. a mistake.

    c. better than returning John Dewey.

ESSAY QUESTION

In 1983, sixteen percent of Florida's teachers failed that state's Teacher Certification Test. Eight students from the Hebrew Day School also took the test. All of them passed the reading section; all but one passed the math section. The students claimed the Certification Test was the easiest test they had ever taken.

Consider this information as you discuss the question: "Should prospective teachers be required to take Hebrew, or will a few words of Yiddish be enough to get by?"

SCORING

If you stooped so low as to answer any of these questions, you are clearly not competent to teach. But DO NOT GET DISCOURAGED. There are still numerous jobs open to you in education as a coordinator, supervisor, project director, curric-

---

Don't Be a Teacher: Be a Euphemism

If you are going to move up in the education profession, you are not going to do it as a teacher. You need a title, and to get that, you need an education specialty. Randomly combine words from columns 1, 2, 3, and 4 and you'll open up whole new career vistas:

1	2	3	4
on-site	criterion	mainstreaming	director
ethnic	behavioral	orientation	evaluator
alphaphonic	outcome-based	enrichment	coordinator
multisensory	learning	proficiency	facilitator
edukinestic	cross-age	assessment	manager
cognitive	remediation	mode	specialist
neurolinguistic	self-image	program	resource person
interdisciplinary	competency	inventory	consultant
minimum	accountability	task	trainer
maximum	basal	curriculum	team leader

ulum specialist, resource person, or consultant. And more positions and new titles all the time!

What Will Happen During Your First Year of Teaching?

The first time you order a film projector, it will arrive with the adaptor plug missing. You will not yet have learned that the adaptor plug is always missing.

You will become well known as an easy touch for candy sales, car-wash tickets, and walkathon contributions.

You will receive a touching love letter from a student you have hardly noticed who will tell you how embarrassed he or she is to be writing a letter like this. The student will leave out either one of the *r*'s or one of the *s*'s in "embarrassed."

At the end of a particularly chaotic day, your most diligent student will stay after class to say, "You should be meaner."

You will find written on a desk: "Ms. X is a bitch." As you are Ms. X, you will not be able to stop crying for two hours.

A seasoned teacher will say to you, "You couldn't possibly have that many A and B students."

If you begin your first semester by announcing, "Sit anywhere you want," you will begin your second semester with a seating chart made out before the first day of school.

Three parents will tell you their children never had a bit of trouble until this year.

You'll feel a twinge of jealousy as you listen to the enthusiastic laughter from Mr. Jackson's classroom. (Would you be less impressed to know it is Mr. Jackson's open fly, not his ready wit, that is generating the uproar?)

When you call your first parent on the telephone, the number will no longer be in service. You will take this incident as a metaphor.

The wild kid who never comes to class will reverse his attendance, if not his behavior pattern, on the first day the principal visits your classroom.

In a recurring dream, the vice-principal, holding your ex-lover firmly in tow, will knock on your bedroom door, demanding, "Why is this student in the hall without a pass?"

On the Saturday morning on which you have agreed to attend a student's piano recital, you will wake up with the second worst hangover of your life. You will go anyway.

A Sampling of Teacherspeak

Here's a chance to show you are a real pro in the teaching biz. Translate the following teacher jargon into English.

It began to rain, and I knew the kids would be *high* when I got off *zoo duty*. I considered working out a different lesson, but I knew one of the *Cecils* and the *Crank* would be hogging the machines, and anyway, I'm a *Group Three* when it comes to machines.

Translation:

High here has nothing to do with the injection of natural or chemical substances. *High* is a type of excited or excitable group behavior induced in students by rain, assemblies, and the last weeks of school; as in:

"My kids are getting higher every day now that we have only——weeks of school left."

Zoo duty refers to the teacher's assignment to supervise the yard or cafeteria during lunch or recess, as in:

"You wanna go to lunch?"

"I can't. I got zoo duty."

Cecil, from Cecil B. DeMille, refers to a teacher who is always, it seems, showing movies. A teacher who sees another teacher pushing a movie projector down a corridor might ask:

"What's playing today, Cecil?"

A *Crank* is the teacher who is always cranking materials out on the ditto machine:

"I guess I better go run this ditto."

"You're going to have to wait; the Crank is at it again."

Group Three is used in reference to anyone who is inept at a given skill:

"I'm a Group Three when it comes to my backhand."

The expression derives from the practice of dividing students into three reading groups: Group Ones being the best readers, Group Threes the worst.

What You Need to Know About In-Service Education

In-service courses, the ones teachers take to improve their professional competence and to advance their pay from skimpy yearly amounts like $14,783 to near-profligate sums such as $15,502, are often more fun than pre-service courses because teachers are able to choose their in-service courses. Thus, the principle of the free market operates, and the professor who talks too much about "interactive relationships" and "multivariant academic models" will soon find no demand for her supply.

Often, in-service credit may be earned at all-day conferences. Here is a sampling of topics covered in such conferences. As the topics suggest, participants would be well advised to bring along their own boots and shovels:

- *Mainstreaming for Fish*
- *Everything You Always Wanted*

to Know About Chalk but Were Afraid to Ask
- *Theory and Practice of Potty Passes*
- *The Art of Managing Milk Money*
- *Developing Criterion Reference Tests for Papier-Mâché Projects*
- *Using Newspaper Horoscopes to Assess Student Needs*
- *Taking the Politics Out of Spelling Bees*
- *Educationese as a Second Language*

Select An Effective Teaching Style

Once upon a time, teachers were in charge of their own classrooms. When they closed their schoolroom doors, they were free to try out any lesson plan, from the orthodox to the kinky. But the Era of Accountability has changed this.

Now: "The student will be able to use end-of-sentence punctuation—the period, the question mark, the exclamation point—with ninety-eight-percent accuracy," say the writers of objectives. While objectives of this sort have a tone that suggests they should be delivered in a German accent by someone wearing a monocle, teachers need not be intimidated. Sure, the Board of Education wants kids to know what kind of marks to put at the end of a sentence, but *how* you teach this skill is up to you.

Here are some student assignments, projects, and activities designed to demonstrate that teachers with different educational styles can all effectively teach about periods, question marks, and exclamation points:

Eleven Ways to Teach Punctuation

Teaching Style #1:
Back to Basics. Copy pages 138 to 142 in your McGuffey's Reader (1984 edition). Underline every period once, every question mark twice, and every exclamation point three times. Do not ask why you are doing this.

Teaching Style #2:
Affective Education. Write a story about how you are feeling about writing a story about your feelings. Substitute exclamation points in sentences you would normally end with a period. Now get in touch with how you feel about all these exclamation points.

Teaching Style #3:
Values Clarification. Imagine that an exclamation point, a question mark, and a period are in a life raft stranded at sea. As the situation worsens, it is decided that the least socially useful mark must jump over the side. Which of the three marks should jump first? Which next? Why?

Teaching Style #4:
Role Playing. Role-play an exclamation point while your partner role-plays a period. Each of

you should argue that you can best punctuate the sentence, "I awoke this morning to find myself transformed into a giant insect(.) (!)"

Teaching Style #5:
Basic Skills Through Art. Make a papier-mâché model of the sentence, "What Is Art?" Punctuate the sentence correctly with a papier-mâché question mark. Display your work. Hide nearby and listen for comments about your creation that could be punctuated with exclamation points.

Teaching Style #6:
The Field Trip. Visit a location where question marks are particularly important, such as a court of law ("Where were you on the night of . . .?"), or a product-research firm ("Do you ever eat potato chips when you watch television?"). Interview people who work at these places about why they need question marks to do their jobs properly. Report to the class.

Teaching Style #7:
The Great Books Curriculum. Write a Socratic dialogue in which you explore all aspects of the question, "Is the exclamation point compatible with the Good Life?"

Teaching Style #8:
Discovery Learning. Take your copy of *Silas Marner*, and in one chapter, white out all the periods, question marks, and exclamation points. Now try reading the chapter again. Is it as much fun to read this time as it was the first time?

Teaching Style #9:
Media Education. Supply end-punctuation marks for a sampling of sentences you hear spoken on television. What differences do you notice between the punctuation of the "CBS Evening News," reruns of "Gilligan's Island," and car-lot commercials that run after 10:00 P.M.?

Teaching Style #10:
Right-Brain Education. Suppose works of art had end-punctuation marks. How would you punctuate the *Mona Lisa*, *Guernica*, and an Andy Warhol Campbell's soup can?

Teaching Style #11:
Relevant and Groovy Research. Investigate and write a report on "The Era of the Great Rock-and-Roll Question Mark from the Lovin' Spoonfuls' 'Do You Believe in Magic?' to Jimi Hendrix's 'Are You Experienced?'"

Master the Great Teacher Clichés

Traditions make modern kids feel secure. Now, you can take advantage of this need adolescents have to connect with the past by mastering the Great Teacher Clichés, those hackneyed remarks with which your teachers and your parents' teachers filled what would otherwise have been dead air. Students today, as much as those of yesteryear, expect to hear classic bromides such as: *"When you get to (fill in anything from second grade to the Princeton Institute for Advanced Studies), they are going to expect you to know (fill in anything from the difference between "who" and "whom" to the names of the kings of ancient Assyria)."*

So don't disappoint your students: Use clichés. But before you uncork your favorite vintage expressions, make sure you consider the truths behind them. Here's some help:

★★

THE GREAT CLICHÉ	THE TRUTH

★★

I'm willing to stay here all night with you people, if you don't quiet down.	Oh my God! How could I say that?

★ ★ ★

You know, the teachers don't make the rules here.	Ve iss juust caryink aut orduhrs.

★ ★ ★

This will definitely be on the exam.	Will somebody please wake up?

★ ★ ★

I am interested in quality, not quantity.	Why should I read three hundred words of illiteracies when you have already established your ignorance in one hundred?

★ ★ ★

I wouldn't give you this if I didn't think you could do it.	I wouldn't give you this if I didn't *hope* you could do it.

★ ★ ★

You might want to take a few notes as I speak.	So if the vice-principal comes in, it will look like we are at least going through the motions.

★ ★ ★

Don't worry about it. It won't be on the exam.

I can't do this problem either.

★ ★ ★

Ten years from now, you'll thank me for that C.

But I kind of hope you don't know where to find me.

★ ★ ★

Now, go to work, you know what you have to do.

Just don't ask why you're doing it.

★ ★ ★

I didn't give you that C; you earned it.

And at minimum-wage rates, to boot.

How to Survive a Faculty Meeting

Maybe teachers don't spend more of their lives attending faculty meetings than they do making love; maybe it just seems that way. In any event, here are some ways teachers have learned to maintain their dignity and self-respect as they sit in cafeterias across the country and listen to vice-principals drone on about how everyone needs to keep lesson plans in the upper-right-hand drawers of his or her desk:

1. Imagine the principal with no clothes on. But dwell on this vision at your own risk.
2. Check out the earlobes of everyone in the room.
3. Pass around a pool selling chances on the exact minute the meeting will adjourn.
4. Ask one of these always relevant questions:
   • Why do we have to reinvent the wheel?
   • Isn't the basic problem one of articulation?
   • May I play devil's advocate for a moment?
   • Isn't this only the tip of the iceberg?
5. Write a passionate note to the member of the faculty you would most like to sleep with.
6. Tear it up.
7. Do an A-to-Z list using the first names of students currently in your classes. It's OK to skip Q and X.
8. Pick a nice word like "viable." Give yourself a point for each time it comes up during the meeting.
9. Make up some little Zenish paradoxes: "Am I in this meeting,

or only dreaming I am in this meeting, or only wishing I was dreaming I was in this meeting, or dreaming I was only wishing . . .?" You get the idea.

10. Make a list of people not present and fantasize exotic excuses for their absence. "Ms. Thingwig has abducted that second-string quarterback from her sixth-period class, and at this moment, has him chained to a bed post at the Holiday Inn."

11. Send a note to a latecomer that says, "Too bad you weren't here earlier to defend yourself."

12. Make categories and put everyone in the room into them: those who would be better off married and those who wouldn't; those who would subscribe to the Playboy Channel if they could afford it, and those who wouldn't; etc.

13. Take verbatim notes of the meeting and send them to William Safire.

A Guide to Classroom Discipline

If your classroom looks like the one depicted on pages 32–33, help is on the way. We now have *Effective Discipline Consultants*. The Effective Discipline Consultant is usually a burnt-out teacher who has retreated from the combat zone to the Gold Room of your local Ramada Inn, where, in exchange for a day's pay (yours), he dispenses "strategies" for coping with children who are "acting out."

While the strategies offered by the Effective Discipline Consultant vary, they do have one thing in common: They don't work. Below are strategies that *do* work:

Call the office and ask someone with a deep voice to recite the Ten Commandments over the school intercom.

Give everyone a library pass, then lock the door from the inside.

Organize a lesson around a demonstration that will touch on a common interest of all the students: a fight to the death between two pit bulls, for instance.

Take the class on a field trip to the Bermuda Triangle. Make sure you get off before the plane leaves.

Tell the students that if they stop screwing up, they may one day be eligible for parole.

Put up a sign that reads "Bedlam Asylum, 1783" and invite the principal in to view your historical tableau.

Try to get some of the Virgos transferred to another section.

Pipe nitrous oxide in through the heating ducts.

 Tell the class to pay attention while you explain the new miracle cure for zits.

 Hire as teacher's aides the three runners-up in the Mr. T. Look-Alike Contest.

 Apply for federal disaster relief.

 Tell the class about the time you slept with James Dean.

 Hire Doug Hennings to make the class disappear; if you can't afford that, have him make you disappear.

 See your travel agent.

Are You Out of Control?

The school system has a way of turning nice, middle-class conformists into raging wackos. No one is immune. One moment you'll be routinely filling out your "Request for an Order Request Form," and the next moment you'll be trying to eat the chalk tray. So pay attention to these clues that suggest you may be losing your grip:

You read over old administrative memos, looking for insights into the meaning of life.

During in-class study periods, you spend most of your time staring at the travel-poster view of Sri Lanka that covers the window of your classroom door.

You suddenly begin to savor the coffee in the school cafeteria.

You resolve to continue your lesson on "lay" and "lie" until everyone gets it.

You find yourself increasingly obsessed by your belief that if all students would only memorize Boyle's law, the world would be a far better place in which to live.

You think your free period is a free period.

You just do not understand why you are the only one who checked 173 copies of *Ivanhoe* out of the bookroom.

You think your honors class needs you.

You throw caution to the wind and request two staplers in one semester.

You spend your lunch period riding the school elevator, singing little songs, like Ophelia.

It does not occur to you that "Back-to-School Night" will conflict with "Remington Steele."

How to Recover from a <u>Real</u> Bad Day

No grab bag of homilies is guaranteed to resurrect our spirits after one of those days that starts with epoxy glue in the keyhole of a classroom door and ends with Sheila Roberti, who knows nothing about opera and cannot carry a tune, enacting the mad scene from *Lucia di Lammermoor* during seventh period.

But we have all worked out our little solutions. Some need to make small bittersweet jokes. Pass on to one of these teachers some Wise Person's maxim like "Education is a progressive discovery of our own ignorance," and you'll get back, "Right, and my students are making *rapid* progress." Tell her you have heard some deep thinker claim that "Teachers should have maximum authority and minimum power"; she'll snap, "Well, at least we're halfway there." Then she'll smile.

Then there are those teachers who get along by not expecting too much. They could see themselves as candidates for the Rick Bosetti Fan Club. Rick Bosetti just happened to be the Oakland Athletics outfielder who asked to be released from his contract at the end of the 1982 season: "I am realistic enough to know I am in the twilight of a mediocre career," he said. The Rick Bosettis of schoolteaching derive a certain strength from the courage to admit they are ordinary.

But if you are like most of us, you are neither a cynic nor a fatalist.

In fact, you are likely an incurable optimist. Like farmers, you believe that no matter how bad things are, next year they'll be better. No doubt you also believe that anyone who is always at his best is always mediocre. It does not surprise you to find out that even Ted Williams never batted more than .400 in any one season, and you know it is certainly no harder to hit a ball coming at you at ninety miles an hour than it is to turn a TV-sotted generation on to the pleasures of *Great Expectations*.

So don't dwell on what went wrong today. Focus instead on those magic moments when everything worked: On the moment Hector Mendoza squirmed with delight because the two of you had just figured out long division; on the time the bell rang during the impassioned discussion of capital punishment and kids' eyes said, "Do we have to go?" Think about these times, and you'll be ready for tomorrow.

The Student Reporter Asks:

Will you please tell us your innermost secrets? Be specific.

"Innermost secret #1: I bleed.

"Innermost secret #2: Every time I mail a letter, I open the lid a second time to see if my letter *really* went down the slot.

"Innermost secret #3: I have thought about strangling many of you.

"Innermost secret #4: I miss many of you so much sometimes that I take out old yearbooks, look at your pictures, and cry."

—A secretive teacher

3

Teacher Types: A Field Guide to Various Subspecies

For many, teacher-watching has become a diverting hobby. Unlike doctors (who cannot be found on Wednesdays), and lawyers (who cannot be found between the hours of twelve and three), teachers can be spotted any day of the week at any time. Truly amusing teacher-watching takes place on snowy weekday mornings at dawn. Just peek out your window and in a few minutes you will see some sad soul trying to jump-start a '67 Volkswagen. That's a teacher. Note the look of anxiety as the teacher tries to decide whether to get in the car and brave the snowdrifts (in which case school is sure to be canceled) or whether to get back in bed (in which case school is sure to be held).

To differentiate among the many different types of teachers, you must first determine whether the teacher you have spotted is male or female. To assist you, diagrams of both sexes have been supplied. Next, read through the listings of subspecies described in this chapter. In no time

at all, you will be able to distinguish between a Red-Headed Male Layback and a Blue-Eyed Female Nerd. Have fun!

Teachers are the ones who...

...quote *Junior Scholastic* at parties.

...ask for separate checks.

...say "Shhh" when they are interrupted.

...always pick up on sexual *double entendres* (and for that reason would never serve a hot dog to a boy over the age of six).

Your Basic Male Teacher

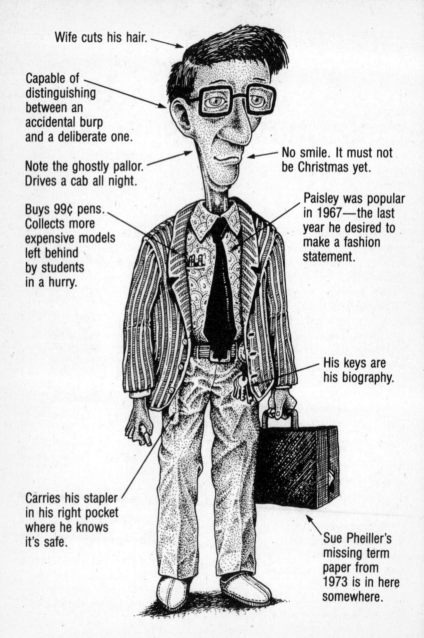

Wife cuts his hair.

Capable of distinguishing between an accidental burp and a deliberate one.

Note the ghostly pallor. Drives a cab all night.

Buys 99¢ pens. Collects more expensive models left behind by students in a hurry.

No smile. It must not be Christmas yet.

Paisley was popular in 1967—the last year he desired to make a fashion statement.

His keys are his biography.

Carries his stapler in his right pocket where he knows it's safe.

Sue Pheiller's missing term paper from 1973 is in here somewhere.

Your Basic Female Teacher

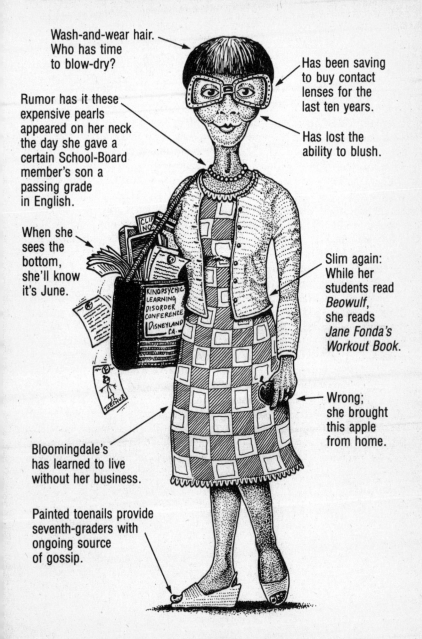

Wash-and-wear hair. Who has time to blow-dry?

Has been saving to buy contact lenses for the last ten years.

Rumor has it these expensive pearls appeared on her neck the day she gave a certain School-Board member's son a passing grade in English.

Has lost the ability to blush.

When she sees the bottom, she'll know it's June.

Slim again: While her students read *Beowulf*, she reads *Jane Fonda's Workout Book*.

Wrong; she brought this apple from home.

Bloomingdale's has learned to live without her business.

Painted toenails provide seventh-graders with ongoing source of gossip.

KINOPSYCHIC LEARNING DISORDER CONFERENCE DISNEYLAND CA-

CLIF NO

TEACHUR

The Mom

The giveaway is that she always says "my kids," never "the class" or "the students." She's the one who always has the box of Kleenex on her desk and who pays the library fine for the kid who can't afford it. On the playground, she knows instinctively when someone is going to crowd in line for the ball and she moves into the breach with the speed of Wonder Woman.

Though she exudes warmth, she can inspire awe: Her "kids" realize she will always know who picked his nose and wiped his boogers in the new reading text. When a piranha is set loose in a classroom aquarium, you can be sure it is not her classroom aquarium.

Certain things she believes to be true (in the face of all evidence to the contrary): hot food is better for kids than cold food; a student can learn to spell a word by writing it exactly ten times—nine won't be enough, and eleven will be busy-work; and if she could have had that kid in her class for one more semester, he might not have turned up on the Ten Most Wanted List fifteen years later.

She is still eager to improve her skills and is often seduced into taking in-service workshops with titles like "Brainstorming with Chalkboards." But the day she caught herself saying, "Monetary emphasis should be placed at K–2 levels," when she meant to say, "Let's put more money into early education," she knew she had had enough professional enrichment for awhile.

If you were ever taught by a Mom, you'll always bear her mark. Even when you are fifty years old, if you are ever tempted to taste a strawberry in your grocery's produce department, you will hear a not-so-still, not-so-small voice say, "I wouldn't have expected this of you, Marjorie." You will decide you are not hungry.

"Okay, everybody, hit the library.
I'll see you in eight weeks."

Mr. Layback

Mr. Layback does not believe much in school. "Nothing worth knowing can be taught," he'll pontificate when he's had a few beers. But Mr. Layback needs to eat, so he has worked out his own compromise: Make the academic ordeal as painless as possible for everyone concerned. That's why he likes to put his students to work on "projects." Here is his lesson plan for the semester.

Weeks 1–9: During class time, students research projects in the school library.
Weeks 10–18: Students present projects orally in class.

When an administrator suggested that perhaps Mr. Layback was not giving his students enough direction, Mr. Layback passed out a bibliography entitled, "Books on Social Sciences and the Humanities," which he had cadged off a college roommate twenty years before. Few of the books listed in the bibliography are actually in the school library, but that does not bother Mr. Layback's students because most of them elect to do "original research." For this research, they are required to ask their classmates and other "subjects" probing questions such as, "If you started to lose your hair, would you get a toupee?" and then report their findings "scientifically." Mr. Layback says that a scientific report is one that takes up at least one-half hour of class time.

When Mr. Layback is required to give a test, we know how he will behave. On the day before the test, he will say, "Test tomorrow." The students will say, "Awwwh." He will say, "OK, then, Friday." On the day of the test, he will take the first fifteen minutes of class to correct the typographical errors on the test: "On number 7, I left out letter D, Ex post facto. That's e-x-"

On the day after the test, reviewing the answers, he will give everybody as much credit as possible. "On number 13, I had in mind A— George Washington was the father of his country—but you're right, I did say that Benjamin Franklin had a lot of illegitimate children, so I'll take D."

There are days when Mr. Layback is not so easygoing. Maybe he's a little hung over or he missed breakfast. On these days, he'll start a detention list for the real and imagined offenders of rules he made up that morning. But then, he'll remember a 3:00 P.M. dental appointment and the culprits will get "one more chance."

"To tell you the truth,
I'd rather read
about it than do it."

The Woman of Letters

Her great regret is that she has not yet been able to visit Emily Dickinson's birthplace and thus pay homage to her spiritual twin. Her Central High School classroom has become her retreat from which she contemplates—in a world gone mad—the wonders of parallel structure and William Butler Yeats.

Decades of "fashionable" educational reform have washed past her; she would no sooner teach a minicourse than she would wear a miniskirt. When she hears talk of computer "literacy" at faculty meetings, she allows herself a wry smile: This, too, will pass.

For seventeen years, students have whispered rumors of her imminent death from a rare liver disease. But she does not listen to these tales. When one knows Jane Austen, one does not care about petty gossip.

In the classroom, the long pause is important to her teaching style. Reading aloud a Shakespeare sonnet, she compacts the energy in her small frame to perform with the full-bosomed histrionics of a modern Sarah Bernhardt. And then she stops—silently fixing each student with a look that says, "You have just heard from God."

The Woman of Letters is a failed author. She understands the cause of her ill fortune: The publishers have decided that because she is "just a teacher," she cannot possibly be a literary genius to boot. If she had spent her life "hobnobbing" with editors at Elaine's, things might have been different.

People remember the time a colleague, irritated by her "elitism," put a note in her box: "*Valley of the Dolls* is the best-selling novel in the history of the world."

"Of course," she replied.

She has a recurring dream in which she is found dead one morning in her classroom. Her head is on her desk and she has drowned in a pool of red ink that has dripped from a pen with which she has scrawled, one last time, "Cite your sources."

The Polyester Playboy

Right off, in his first year of teaching, the Polyester Playboy realized he was different. He was the only one at the faculty party who knew the cha-cha-cha. Now, like his favorite singer, he does it his way. He is not going to be one of those teachers who count nickels toward some supersaver economy package tour of ancient ruins, available only to those who book four years in advance and share toothbrushes. Oh, no. When vacation comes for him, he parties in Vegas, an excursion even his Mafioso tax man has never had the nerve to write off as educational.

He tries to live a little during the rest of the year, too, often showing up bleary-eyed on Monday mornings after a wild weekend with one of his "ladies," out splurging on two-for-one tickets at all-you-can-eat smorgasbords. It is on these mornings that he shows his class an "El Flicko." "Any El Flicko will do," he says to the librarian. "Give me *Dolly Madison: America's First Cupcake*. Give me *Defensive Driving for Offensive People*. I just want to turn the lights off and not talk."

Though committees are not normally his thing, he has become a vocal member of the Textbook Selection Committee. Here he lobbies for a text with lots of questions at the ends of the chapters, an educational tool he needs on those mornings when his mouth tastes like old socks.

This is not to say he never teaches. When he has had a good night's sleep, he relishes telling his class the story of this or that battle, interspersing little *double entendres* like "It's the man behind the gun that counts," and then waiting for embarrassed snickers.

Once recently, tired of lying to stewardesses in Airport Hilton bars about his career as a real estate developer, he decided to write a personal ad. He got to the part about being "a professional man" and realized it wasn't going to fly.

"What can I say?
When a fellow's got
his two-for-oners at
Ponderosa Steak House,
he's never hard up
for a date."

"Come on, let's get serious! Now, how many of you think I should get my hair cut?"

Just One of the Kids

She's a little bit embarrassed about winning the students' favorite-teacher poll six years in a row, but what can she do about it? *Catcher in the Rye* really *is* her favorite novel. She *believes* those weighty literary interpretations such as, "When a writer makes everything red, he has sex on his mind."

In grammar class, she likes to make up sentences in which she is the subject and either Tom Selleck or Harrison Ford is the object. Or sometimes even the other way around.

She marks papers with unrestrained enthusiasm, employing superlatives more commonly associated with movies like *Raiders of the Lost Ark* than with juvenile ramblings about *The Scarlet Letter:* "Fantastic Point!" "Fabulous Idea!" A student knows he has displeased her when he gets back a paper with only a single happy face (☺). When students *do* please her—which is most of the time—she loves to have junk food parties in her classroom. She would consider it a violation of her academic freedom were the principal to curtail these sugar orgies.

She thinks soap operas help people solve their problems, and she was appalled recently when a class of juniors could not recall a single episode of "Ryan's Hope." The school librarian, who normally is willing to subscribe to any magazine, from *Cat Fanciers' News* to *Muscle International*, adamantly refuses to order *Soap Opera Digest*. So she has improvised. Her life has become the students' soap opera. Instead of turning to "General Hospital" each morning, students turn in to Room 239, where they hear their teacher's real-life story about her sister who is after her aunt's money and about the rich guy she met at the party who refused to come in for coffee but who was too old for her anyway and probably married.

Sometimes she thinks maybe she needs to see a shrink, but the kids don't think she needs to see anyone. To them, she is an endangered species: a teacher who is still a person.

The Nerd

These days, with all kinds of weird, computer-rich nuts in the news, talk in the teachers' lounge has it that the Nerd's life might have been different—that anyone as dorkey as he is must be a genius. Unfortunately, the only silicon the Nerd knows about is the kind girls used to enlarge their breasts back in the days when "The Beverly Hillbillies" was his favorite television show.

The Nerd has not had many honors in his life, unless you count being the only person on the faculty to have locked his keys in his car so many times that the American Automobile Association has canceled his membership.

On most days, the Nerd brings to his classes a not-particularly-admirable consistency. In his grammar class, he regularly parses the sentences "Jack hit the ball" and "Jill was going to the store." In math class, it is always Bill who has nine apples (they are always apples) and who gives Dick two of them. If Jack or Bill or Dick has a dog, it will be named (right) Spot. The Nerd has named his own dog Spot in honor of these sentences.

The Nerd also gives a lot of seatwork in which kids copy from the text answers to questions, so he normally carries around stacks of papers "to be graded." He grades these papers with a single check, which means (he tells his students), "I have looked at this." Sometimes, if a kid copies more from the book than the other kids and writes very neatly, the Nerd will give a check-plus ($\checkmark +$) which means, "I have looked at this. Very good."

Over the years, the Nerd has made an effort. For a while he sponsored the bowling club, but gave it up when a bowling ball fell on his foot and some administrator refused him worker's compensation. Once he brought his favorite Mitch Miller album to school for an end-of-the-term class party, but the kids ripped it off and he had to buy it back at a garage sale. Another time, after taking a summer education course, "How to Have Creative Spelling Bees," he tried to have one. But they never taught him in that course what to do about kids who keep sneaking back in line. So he quit experimenting.

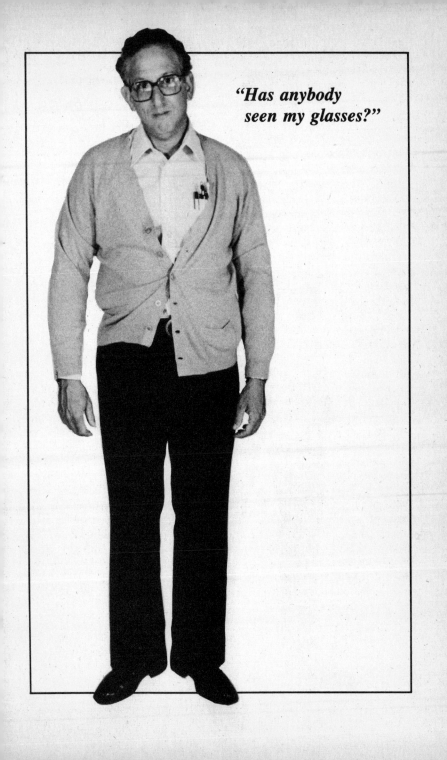

The Man with a Cause

He likes to talk about how it was when he went to Kent State in the sixties, a claim his colleagues have the good taste not to press. What he does not want to abolish, he wants to ban. He encourages his students to join his crusades. The posters on the wall of his room announce more "stops" than the signs at a six-way intersection.

He entered teaching with his sixties catechism intact. But he ran into some problems immediately. On the first midterm, he gave every student an A because grades "are just a way of tracking kids into different institutions." No one studied the rest of the semester. Those were the days when he insisted students call him by his first name, Roger, instead of Mr. Bawldridge. Some students compromised with Mr. Roger, just like in *Gone with the Wind*—not what he had in mind.

These days, he limits his working-class solidarity to calling cafeteria workers and substitute janitors by their first names.

And there are signs he is mellowing.

Yes, merit pay is still "divisive," the bell-shaped curve remains "a schematic imposed by the American ruling class," and the senior prom is "a rehearsal for a lifetime of petty-bourgeois consumerism." However, last semester he did agree to chair the schoolwide Good Spelling Committee. Just the right cause for the 1980s.

The Swinging Virgin

Two generations of pubescent teenage boys have admired the Swinging Virgin's legs. She has been told she looks like Angie Dickinson. The trouble is she thinks and talks like Our Miss Brooks, a limitation that has made it possible for her to preserve her chastity on sixty-three ski weekends and four Club Med vacations.

The picture shown here was not taken at school. "School is not a big part of my life," she often says.

But *she* is a big part of school life. The day she left the third button of her blouse open, she knew what it was to be a star. She would not deny she is a bit of a tease. Once some male students presented her with a tee shirt saying, "Teachers Do It in Class." "Bad taste," she admonished. But the next day, she wore her own tee shirt: "Teachers Do It *with* Class."

"You need to learn your prepositions," she cooed.

Yes, she would like to get married, but she is not going to grovel like her girlfriend (whom she found at a dyslexia convention groping around the floor in search of an imaginary contact lens, hoping to pick up an eligible pediatrician).

Lately she has been working on changing her image. She is now more Bergdorf Goodman and less Frederick's of Hollywood. She is trying to cut down on her smoking, and she is thinking about starting work on a counseling credential.

"Dolly Parton, eat your heart out."

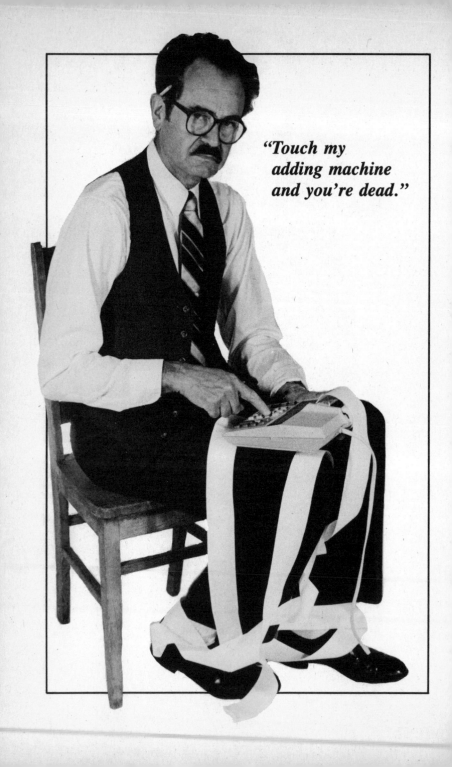

The Record Keeper

If fondling one's grade book in public were a crime, the Record Keeper would be serving a life sentence. He is never seen planning lessons or correcting papers, but he is often seen adding points, feverishly fingering his calculator, smiling as beatifically as a maharishi with a head full of hashish. His life began to improve several years ago when he decided to stop noticing the existence of students. That's when he started "covering." Ask him on the first day of the semester when he'll be "covering" the assassination of President Garfield, he'll tell you; ask him why, and he'll find some numbers to add up.

Knowing his devotion to structure, students vie to ask questions that will divert him from the subject. They know that questions about his World War II experience sometimes work, and questions about World War II C-rations *always* work.

But mostly, the Record Keeper is all business. He devotes the first day of class to an incomprehensible explanation of his method for "factoring out" grades. In practice, the system works out so that everyone, except for a few shills who must be working for the house, misses some higher grade or another by .00085321 of a point. A student who challenges the Record Keeper's grand design enters a thicket of ranks, means, curves, and percentiles, and emerges humbled and grateful that he has been spared that *coup de grâce*: the standard deviation.

Of course, there are compensations for students. The Record Keeper has been using the same exams since the British pulled out of India. So about the second week in June, loose copies of these exams are passed about, generating an interest more commonly reserved for the good parts of books like *The Story of a Dildo*. This kind of activity can play hell with a standard deviation.

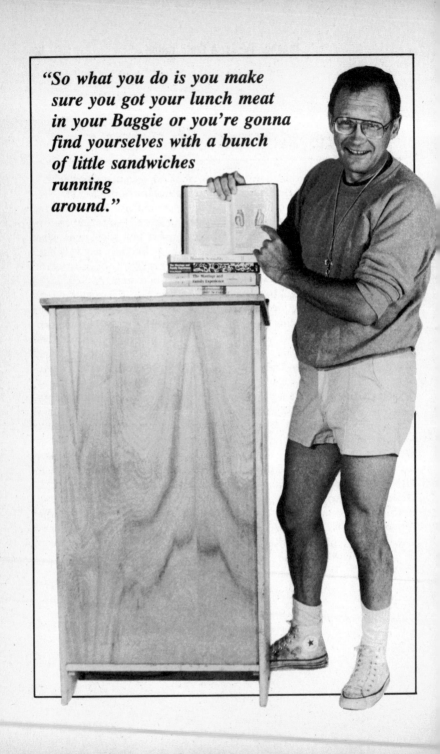

"So what you do is you make sure you got your lunch meat in your Baggie or you're gonna find yourselves with a bunch of little sandwiches running around."

The Jock

Here we do not see the Jock in his natural habitat of sweaty orifices and fag jokes. Rather, we see him as the academic: smirking his way through sex education class. Later in the day, in history, he will be telling his class about the battle of Bunker Hill and how it was really a delay pattern. "Those guys just stood back there in the pocket and waited it out." When he gets to the Battle of Gettysburg, he'll make clear that Pickett's charge "was like sending those wimpy running backs from the old Detroit Lions up the middle against the Pittsburgh Steel Curtain."

As the Jock belongs to the one-damn-thing-after-another school of teaching history, he is not much on sophisticated links or smooth transitions. "Moving right along...," he'll say, and his students know it's time to skip a line in their notebooks as he ends his discussion of the Civil War and jumps eighty years or so to "the big one"—World War II.

The subject the Jock most enjoys teaching is sex education, and in that course he is not embarrassed to mount a soapbox. "Some times you'll get some bozo who doesn't realize he is playing with fire who will go right ahead and dip his schnitzel into some girl's jing-jang without taking any precautions. Bango! There's another one in the oven."

Actually, the Jock is not a bad sort. He's the one who tries to organize the TGIF's, sending out notices in fake-pompous language about how "we need to get together to share some libations and renew our sense of collegiality." He's also the one who circulates the pools at World Series and Super Bowl time. It is not his fault that some substitute cafeteria worker always wins the $200.

"O.K., extra credit: What does it feel like being poor and miserable?"

The Lawyer's Wife

She does not teach because she has to earn a living—and don't you forget it. On good days, she teaches out of noblesse oblige. On bad days she's saving for her own Mercedes 280 SL. In a group of teachers, she's easy to spot. She's the one who drives the only BMW in the teachers' parking lot and brings chocolate truffles to the PTA pot luck. Like many teachers, she furnishes her home in the chic minimalist style, but with her it's a matter of choice, not necessity.

As a new teacher, her first mission was to transport F. Scott Fitzgerald from an ivy-covered school in the middle of Cambridge (where she had learned to love him) to a boarded-window school in the middle of Chicago (where he was so much needed). Chicago is a long way from West Egg, but she was sure her students really did understand Gatsby. They told her about a "dude" on the block who also wore a new shirt every day—and drove a pink Rolls Royce, too.

Now that her husband is out of law school, she teaches in the suburbs—where she invites to her class guest-speaking lesbian activists, ex-cons, unionized prostitutes, and other folks she would not want in her neighborhood after dark.

Her end-of-the-semester "celebrations," as she calls them, have become famous as the annual climactic battleground in her ongoing effort to raise her students' taste. If the students will only listen to Vivaldi's *Gloria* all the way through; if they will only try a bit of tuna sashimi or braised kiwi fruit; then, during the last fifteen minutes of the period, they will be free to play Pink Floyd records and scarf Ho Ho's.

The Dictator

A man who could make the trains run on time, the Dictator has settled for holding students to a schedule. A sign on his desk announces his philosophy of education: NO LATE PAPERS. His lectures, delivered in the manner of a highway patrol officer informing a drunk driver of his rights, are punctuated by wheezes and hacks from students too sick to be at school but afraid to be anyplace other than his classroom.

Though the Dictator goes through the motions of grading exams, students usually learn their grades *during* his tests: He paces the room peering at exam papers, occasionally nodding in approval, more regularly shaking his head in disgust.

Communication is not his specialty. Subscribing to the dictum that students should be neither seen nor heard, he addresses the assembled while maintaining rigid eye contact with the photo of General Patton on the back wall. He normally does not speak to teachers except to say things like, "I think you have my stapler." He does, however, write a lot of notes to counselors, most of which demand that a disruptive student who "asks too many questions" be removed from his class forthwith. However, since he realizes that the "limp-wristed types" who go into counseling only object to questions that could embarrass liberal Democrats, he really does not expect anything will be done.

*"The last time
I smiled was the
day F.D.R. died."*

"Tomorrow,
I'd like each
of you to bring
in a dead cat
or dog."

Mr. Science

The kids like to say that the white coat he wears daily is the same one he wore the day he flunked out of medical school. And although his 2.6 average from Fall River Tech precluded so much as an application to any medical school north of Grenada, his white coat does have a way of saying, "I'm special. I could be making a lot more money fooling around with DNA or passing out samples of epinephrine for Bristol-Myers, but here I stay amidst voltmeters and Bunsen burners, dedicating my life to the youth of America."

Sometimes Mr. Science thinks about what would happen if he did leave. No doubt his classes would fall into the hands of that young teacher down the hall who has never once required her students to label the parts of a crayfish and who herself may not be able to tell the difference between the carapace and the green glands. So Mr. Science sticks with it.

Sure, there have been disappointments. He soon learned that the chemistry that motivates teenagers has little to do with positive ions. But he still enjoys those days when he stands before the class and makes the magnesium smoke and the zinc chloride change from clear to blue. It may not be Doug Hennings, but it's more magic than the kids get elsewhere in school.

Then there are the meaner pleasures he doesn't talk about much. A part of him likes filling the clear bottles with reptile parts and watching the freshmen gross out. He relishes the day the sophomores squirm as they negotiate who gets to read the directions and who actually has to cut up the frog. On test days, he takes a perverse pleasure in asking sneaky questions—like "Who invented the Leyden jar?"—that assure him no student will "top out".

"You're wrong. The answer is not Mr. Leyden; it's Peter Musschenbroek (spelling counts), and you'd better learn that if you ever expect to get into medical school."

The Professional Substitute

This man learned that substituting was for him when he realized that, unlike most of the other two million or so teachers in America, he did not come down with debilitating and communicable diseases on Mondays and Fridays. Besides, what else are you going to do with a degree in Reichian economics?

Each day he expects the worst and is seldom disappointed.

- He is loaned a "pass key" that will not open the classroom door.
- The teacher's lesson plan will say, "Have students continue to read the chapter in the book. Please follow these directions exactly." No student in the class will know what chapter, or even what book, is being referred to. "She usually just lets us discuss things," they will say.
- At 9:02, by prearrangement, all the students in the class will cough in unison.
- At 9:04, a wave of diarrhea and bladder ailments in proportions worthy of attention by the Centers for Disease Control will sweep the classroom.

And that's just first period.

But the Professional Substitute does not let all this get him down. He knows his options.

Sometimes he announces a study period ("Yes, you may talk quietly") and retreats behind the *New York Times* crossword puzzle. He has found this stance quite effective in impressing certain pseudointellectual senior girls who see in the substitute an existentialist outsider, a kind of academic Hell's Angel.

Sometimes he performs a set piece, usually about his own experience, in which he embellishes the debaucheries of his Animal House college days or totally fabricates a story, like the time his buddy, who worked for Motown, got him into a recording session the day Michael Jackson was singing the high notes for Diana Ross.

Sometimes on Friday, but never on Monday, he will interact with students. He'll tell the class that most men have index fingers shorter than their ring fingers and most women have ring fingers shorter than their index fingers. Then he'll set the students loose to find the weirdos whose fingers are different.

In one of his most successful lessons, the Substitute brought in a few rulers and had students test the general principle that the distance from your elbow to your wrist equals the length of your foot.

All this creativity aside, the Substitute knows his real job. He is the relief pitcher of American education, called in to finish a game already lost.

"Why me?"

★★

What Kind of Teacher Are You?

★★

The following quick check will establish your teaching profile. Unless you have tenure, better make sure you keep that profile *low.*

Male or Female?
Will the vice-principal believe you have to leave early for a gynecology appointment?

Ethnic or WASP?
Is the food in the teachers' cafeteria an improvement on what you get at home?

Innovative or Traditional?
Would it be OK with you if the desks in your classroom were bolted to the floor in six rows of five each?

Pessimistic or Optimistic?
Do you believe the principal when he says, "If you'll just take this one more kid, I won't ask you to take any more"?

Young or Old?
When you show a film in class, is it "media" or an "audiovisual aid"?

Sweet or Sour?
When a student returns from an absence, are you more likely to ask, "How are you?" or "Where were you?"

Dedicated or Goof-Off?
When you get around to handing back papers, does one kid say, "Oh, I sorta remember this"?

Organized or Disorganized?
When you tell a kid, "I'm sure I'll be able to find that paper you didn't get back," are you lying?

Competent or Incompetent?
When you return from an absence, do the students often say, "We really learned *a lot* from that substitute"?

Looking for a Bathroom in All the Wrong Places: A Guide to Your School

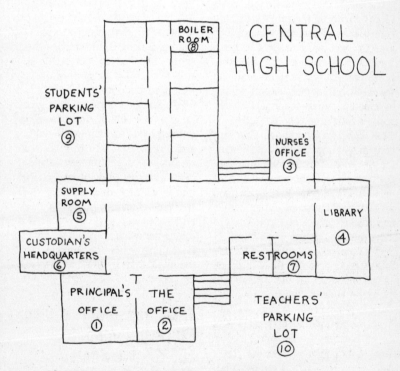

When you arrive at your new teaching job, you'll surely be given a map of the school area that looks much like the one on this page. We have included here some annotations that your principal's orientation session may have neglected.

1. *Principal's Office*. Recent changes in Board of Education policy have declared obsolete the croc-

odile-filled moat that once made teacher access to this space a chore.

2. *The Office*. Bailiwick of the school secretary. Avoid this area if (a) you have not handed in your chicken-pox immunization forms; (b) you have handed them in late; (c) you have failed to alphabetize something; and/or (d) you have generally not functioned according to instructions.

3. *Nurse's Office*. This is a great place for a student to pick up the National Dairy Council's four-color glossy brochure on the joys of milk consumption. However, it is not such a great place for a student to get a Band-Aid. She must be (a) bleeding profusely, (b) waving a consent slip signed by her mother, and (c) willing to donate her body to the physiology class if anything goes wrong.

4. *Library*. Encourage your students to get hooked on books during the eleven days of the year this wonderful facility is not closed for inventory, P.T.A. teas, Faculty Council sessions, achievement testing, grade recording, student government meetings, or termite inspection.

5. *Supply Room*. Open every day from 10:00 A.M. to 10:17 A.M. A partial inventory of the treasures to be found here includes:

hole punchers	987
staple removers	1,432
#2 pencils	3

6. *Custodian's Headquarters*. *Here you will find:* (a) good coffee, (b) the best of Rex Stout and Zane Grey, and (c) a portrait of a Vargas girl (circa 1949).

Here you will not find: the custodian.

7. *Student Restrooms*. Only now are these facilities beginning to be used again after two unsavory decades. Perhaps by 1990 the bladder of a camel will no longer be a requisite for high school graduation.

8. *Boiler Room*. Believed to be the "office" of the "site liaison facilitator," the "trouble-shooting" administrator who spends most of her time in transit between the School Board offices and Central High. A teacher (who not coincidentally believes in Big Foot) claims to have one day spotted the "site liaison facilitator" devouring a pastrami sandwich behind the furnaces in this room. The Faculty Council is considering setting up a hotline to collect further reports.

9. *Students' Parking Lot*. If your idea of the youth of America is epitomized by a Norman Rockwell boy and girl sharing a Coke with a pair of straws, stay away from the students' parking area. Back there it's the wrong kind of coke.

10. *Teachers' Parking Lot*. Parking places are assigned according to the usual pecking order: The fewer keys you are required to carry, the choicer your spot.

Your Classroom: A Nice Place to Fumigate, but You Wouldn't Want to Teach There

There are certain facts of life: The last child born gets the worst clothes; the last person at the supper table gets the worst food; and the last teacher in the school gets the worst classroom. When you arrive at a new school, you can be certain of only one thing: THERE IS SOMETHING HORRIBLY WRONG WITH YOUR CLASSROOM. Be relieved if what is wrong happens to be visible—windows without glass can be boarded up, and roaches can be stepped on. More frightening is the classroom that looks good. If your room has a cheery view, a nice desk, and plenty of shelves, look out. Come winter, you're going to find out that room also has subzero temperatures.

Now is there anything to be done with such a classroom? Yes there is. MAKE FRIENDS WITH YOUR JANITOR.

From the moment you walk into your new school, the janitor of that school becomes the most important person in your life. Even if you're married. Even if you have children of your own. Even if you're a devoutly religious person. Janitors, not principals, control the lives of teachers. Your garbage can is full? Well, tough luck to you if you forgot to say "Good morning" to the janitor one frantic Monday. You say there's a flood in your room and your first-graders are in danger of drowning? Here's hoping you made certain those first-graders picked up after themselves at the close of yesterday's school day, or else . . .

In addition to being able to make your classroom safe (if not attractive), your janitor is able to enhance or destroy your career. Principals—not always the wisest of souls—are wise enough to know that the janitor has the goods on you. Your janitor knows everything there is to know about you just by glancing at your classroom: Papers on the floor? You can't control your students. Gum under the desks? You can't control your students. Handwriting on the desks? You can't control your students. Get the picture? Now, what you must do to prevent your janitor from squealing on you is to befriend that janitor in a big way. When is the janitor's birthday? Does the janitor celebrate Christmas or Chanukah? Whichever, a bottle of bourbon is the traditional gift on these occasions, so up the ante to two bottles, and make sure ther're Jack Daniels.

Yes, you *can* have enough desks for every student in your room.

No, you *don't* need to wear a down coat all winter.

Yes, there *is* chalk to be found.

No, you *don't* have to bring candles so the kids can see when they read. So, next time you see someone carrying a broom in a hallway, don't smile and turn away: Bow.

1. Couch functionally designed to prevent prep period naps.

2. Fly-specked Degas, donated fifteen years ago when a young teacher cleaned out her apartment before quitting teaching to marry a dentist.

3. Table constructed by wood-shop students in the 1960s. Top view would reveal representations of peace symbols and suspicious-looking five-fingered leaves.

4. Chair about to be requisitioned as stage furniture for the senior play and never to be seen again.

5. How does this sink get dirty when no one ever washes anything?

6. This typewriter broke four and a half years ago. Every day since then, at least one teacher has entered the Teachers' Lounge and said, "Is that typewriter fixed yet? I really need to use it."

A Map

7. One of the legs on this Formica table is loose. They take turns.

8. *Objet d'art* left unclaimed by ceramics-class students.

9. Site of the Men's Club daily encampment. Sort of a lower-middle-class Bohemian Grove without the redwoods.

10. The "goddamn" Coke machine tantalizes with eight selections, but delivers only diet Dr. Pepper—occasionally with a cup.

11. This coffee maker has inspired the head of the Social Studies Department to quote Abraham Lincoln: "If this is coffee, please bring me some tea; but if this is tea, please bring me some coffee."

12. The students who put the "Cancer Ward" sign on the door of the Teachers' Lounge were only kidding. That's what they said, anyway.

13. Examine this bulletin board closely. You will find an announcement of a "Mandatory Meeting for Teachers Planning to Retire in June, 1969."

14. This man may be dead, but as they said at the demise of Calvin Coolidge, "How can they tell?"

One-Liners from the Teachers' Lounge

Some harried Friday afternoon, wander into the Teachers' Lounge and you may hear:

"What? You've never had Janice Robocco, the clock-watching champion of the world? Her father told me it's getting to the point where she's timing '60 Minutes.'"

"Here they are in the so-called honors class and they still expect me to explain the problems."

"What do you think? Should I allow André Brown to practice his break dancing during sustained silent reading as long as he doesn't bother anyone?"

"Have you ever had a homework paper DEDICATED to you? What do you think that means?"

"I wonder what would happen if they bought each of us one of those gigantic, view-from-the-fortieth-floor power desks. Can you imagine sitting behind one of those suckers and commanding, 'Hillary, spit out your gum'?"

"I've got so many jocks in my third-period general math class, I'm thinking of installing Astroturf."

"He told me he would write the five-hundred lines but only—quote—on the understanding that this act would not constitute an admission of guilt—unquote."

"Is that kid who got the refund on the mock income-tax return he filled out in consumer math out of jail yet?"

"When I saw the tack on my chair, I said to myself, 'OK, just don't say anything; this could make you a better person!'"

"Hey, some kid just told me I have the same birthday as Mick Jagger!"

"Henry James just doesn't seem to have a hell of a lot to say to my fourth-period class these days."

"She's got a list of Do's and Don'ts that includes everything but the Infield Fly Rule, and still the kids are hanging out the window."

Teachers' Lounge Conversation: A Starter Kit

If you find yourself staying away from the Teachers' Lounge, maybe it's because the conversation is too predictable. Why not take responsibility for changing this leaden atmosphere? We present here some conversation starters guaranteed to have your colleagues at each other's throats in a matter of moments.

In 1978, all hell broke loose in St. Anthony, Idaho, when the School Board tried to prevent John Fogurty from teaching Ken Kesey's *One Flew Over the Cuckoo's Nest*. Fogurty appealed to Kesey and received a reply which read in part, "I object to *Cuckoo's Nest* being taught. What's there to teach? It's an entirely simple work, a book any high school kid can read and comprehend without help. Let *Cuckoo's Nest* alone on the drugstore rack and teach instead *Moby Dick* or *The Sound and The Fury* or works by Dickens or Hardy or Shakespeare, for crying out loud!" Inquire as to whether your colleagues agree or disagree with Mr. Kesey.

In 1983 the School Board at Church Hill, Tennessee, was under heavy pressure from upright citizens to ban the tale of Goldilocks and the Three Bears from the community school. Their argument: The girl *was* breaking and entering and she got off with not so much as a slap on the wrist. What do your fellow teachers have to say about this?

Investigators from the University of Massachusetts conducted experiments in which they had teachers insult students in some classes, telling them that they "had I.Q.'s equal to television sets." The kids in these classes did better on a test of material being taught than a group of kids who had not been similarly insulted. Would your friends in the Teachers' Lounge like to try this experiment out themselves?

In 1982, Barry Singer, who was teaching the "Psychology of Sex" course at California State University, Long Beach, argued the educational benefits of a teacher getting intimately involved with his or her students:
1. "We get detailed, ongoing feedback from the person about his or her classmates and their feelings about the class."
2. "A teacher might feel more like showing off in class, which translates into good teaching."
No comment.

In March 1984, Don Lopez, a teacher of agricultural education at Brentwood High School, Brentwood, California, made the papers when a parent protested his method of offering extra credit. He awarded points to any student who, in front of the class, would castrate a sheep by biting off its testicles. Lopez explained he had been awarding such credit for years. Do your colleagues think his teaching strategy has wider educational implications?

In 1982, Los Angeles Mayor Tom Bradley had an idea whose time has not yet come. He suggested we should find the TV addicts—the kids who run home from school to spend hours with the Plug-In Drug—and keep these students after school in an academic environment, away from the television. He admitted his plan would cost money, but he said, "It would be a better investment than the $12,000-a-year cost of keeping them in prison later." Do your friends in the lounge agree or disagree with Mayor Bradley?

They aren't coddling five-year-olds anymore in Benton Arbor, Michigan. There you will flunk kindergarten unless you can print your first name, recognize basic colors, recite a four-line nursery rhyme, count to twenty, and write any number from zero to ten when asked.

Someone in the lounge will now tell you about two or three tenth-graders who couldn't make it.

Ask the teachers in the lounge what they think of this: At San Diego's Memorial Junior High, students receive twenty-five cents a day (to be spent on school-related items) for every day they are in school. Principal Bob Amparan says of the plan, "I'm not paying kids for coming to school. I'm rewarding them for being in school. There's a subtle distinction."

Ask your English-teacher colleagues which of these two sentences they like better:

"I prefer to live in a large city because there you are free to do things you can't do in a small town."

"My preference is for life in a large city because there I would have the freedom to do things that can't be done in a small town."

Some professors did a study that showed most English teachers preferred the overstated second version. The *professors* preferred the first version.

In Galesburg, Illinois, three college professors calling themselves terrorists of the Cultural Liberation Organization "executed" three freshmen before a mock firing squad because of intellectual apathy.

CLO leaders said the attack at Knox College was triggered by frustration with students who are uninterested in their classes and the world around them.

Authorities said the three faculty members, disguised in paramilitary garb and carrying realistic-looking weapons, burst into an unsuspecting class of freshman students, overturning tables and shouting obscenities.

The "terrorists" lined the entire class up against a wall with their hands and feet spread and picked out three students who had been particularly apathetic and nonparticipatory.

The students were tried by their

classmates on charges of "intellectual apathy" and "crimes against Knox College" before receiving a punishment of death by firing squad.

The convicted students were roped together with their hands behind their back and placed before a brick wall. After the prisoners were blindfolded, the chief terrorist "executed" them with a blank-filled .38-caliber starter's gun.

The professors said the class had one of its best discussions at its next meeting.

Ask if your fellow teachers would like to have such a mock execution.

A few years ago a fellow named Ken Musko developed a "Teacher Enthusiasm Renewal" course, which burnt-out teachers could take for a price. Among the activities they experienced in the course:

- They warmed up by making really loud "Oh" sounds.
- They rappeled off the roof of the school down the wall of the building.
- They soared a hundred feet into the air using a parachute.
- Ten of them found a way to climb onto a round disk two feet in diameter.

They returned to the classroom ready for anything.

Ask your colleagues if they would sign up for Mr. Musko's class.

11:05 A.M. at Central High

When it comes to describing what goes on at your school, you, like most teachers, are probably a lot like the blind man describing the elephant. You have intimate knowledge of the leg you happen to be clutching, but the Big Picture eludes you. Join us as we visit Central High and observe some of the little dramas erupting at 11:05 on a typical day:

- Dede Daskin squirms in French class, trying to remember how to say, "Can I go to the toilet?" *en français*.
- The new earth-science teacher asks the vice-principal if he'll spend a few hours with her helping her improve her "eye contact," a skill he found deficient last time he observed her class.
- In the main hallway, a male P.E. teacher stops a member of the faculty Social Committee and suggests the committee is "piddling away" the faculty-meeting treat fund on "nuts and berries."
- A mother phones the counseling office and demands that the biology teacher release her son from class so the boy can hold his mother's place in the line for Bruce Springsteen tickets.
- The principal ponders taking action against the school newspaper, which has just published a caricature of him bearing a

not-altogether-coincidental resemblance to Idi Amin.

- Mr. Reingold, the civics teacher, places a note in the drama teachers' mailbox making it clear that he will no longer allow the star of the senior play to send her understudy to take notes in his class.

- A group of chemistry students, their tests just returned, emit the anxious cry of the red-inked grade grubber: Wadjaget? Wadjaget? Wadjaget?

- In an empty classroom, Jerome Gray faces a blackboard and writes "Please Save!!" above a very small chalk drawing he has labeled: "Mr. Gildersleeve's pecker."

- An emergency meeting of the Faculty Council convenes to discuss the question, "Where does all the chalk go?"

- The Math Department head negotiates a dispute between two teachers who have arrived at the ditto machine at the same moment.

- Stephanie Hallwood applies herself to her "extracurricular" wood-shop project: building fake lavatory passes which she will sell at the going rate.

- In the Teachers' Lounge, Ms. Thrumgood uses her preparation period to complete Lesson Six of the Travel Agents of the World Correspondence Course.

- As students copy last night's algebra homework on the board, Mr. Hanson daydreams about running away from home to pursue a career dealing blackjack in Atlantic City.

- Seven visitors from Japan uncase their Nikons and snap pictures in Ms. Heilbrom's economics class, as if they were voracious paparazzi and Ms. Heilbrom were Jackie O.

- A monitor interrupts Mr. Wentworth's driver education class with an emergency announcement: Victor French is to be excused immediately to pick up supplies for the Fencing Club candy sale.

5

How to Succeed in Teaching Without Really Trying

The notion that teaching is a complicated skill is a false one promulgated by education professors who want to keep you signing up for in-service courses that hold out hope—however faint—that you can learn THE SECRET OF SUCCESSFUL TEACHING.

Now it is no longer necessary to waste your time and money on these courses. By following the advice in this chapter, you can become the World's Greatest Teacher...effortlessly.

How to Become the World's Greatest Teacher: Ten Easy Steps to Success

1. Set and consistently enforce firm rules...*that are flexible.*
2. When you need help with a disruptive student, ask for it. Administrators are there to aid you in dealing with behavior problems...*and to give you low evaluations when they find out you cannot control your class.*
3. Be enthusiastic and energetic ...*remembering all the while that teaching is not a personality contest.*
4. Encourage students to help each other...*except on test days and other times that really count.*
5. Allow students to learn at their own pace...*as long as they are all performing at grade level when standardized-test time comes around.*
6. Impress on students that they are responsible for their own behavior...*and that you will call their parents the first time they mess up.*
7. Encourage spontaneity...*by regularly scheduling creative activities.*
8. Remember you need a private life...*to present yourself as a role model to your students and the community.*
9. Understand that each student is a unique individual...*who can only be understood in terms of*

her very own mean score on the Springer-Worthstein *Personality Index*.

10. Urge your students to act their age . . . *but hope they don't take you literally.*

Use Sex to Liven Up Your Classroom

Most every American advertiser, with the possible exception of the makers of Preparation H, has learned that sex sells products. It follows that teachers—sellers of concepts, ideas, and spelling rules—can very well put sex to work for them as they peddle the possessive apostrophe and other keys to the good life. But be careful.

Use Only What Works for You

One aging math teacher engages his students with the following problem:

If the average man spends 9 hours of his life experiencing sexual climax, what percentage of his lifetime does a man who lives to 72 spend having orgasms?

Much intellectual excitement here; no complaints.

Yet when his much younger colleague down the hall tried the same problem, the fellow found himself reassigned to a job counting protractors at the supply warehouse.

Choose Your Information Carefully

Here are two facts. Which one is the more appropriate subject matter for an eighth-grade math problem?

a. A person engaged in a wild, acrobatic sexual encounter may burn up to 320 calories.

b. A person kissing with his or her mouth closed may burn up to 6 calories.

If you answered *B*, you are correct. It is always a good idea to use low numbers when introducing students to new mathematical concepts.

Try to Get Sex into As Many Areas of the Curriculum As Possible

Some examples:

ECONOMICS

If red M & M's, commonly considered aphrodisiacs, are in shorter supply than the less sexually charged chocolate-covered variety, which candy will bring the higher price on the free market?

GEOGRAPHY

When American men were asked, "Have you had any sexual thoughts in the last five minutes?" thirty-seven percent said "Yes." In Ghana, sixty-five percent answered "Yes." How many time zones does a resident of Denver, Colorado, need to travel through to reach Ghana?

PSYCHOLOGY

True or False: *If you dream about doughnuts and cucumbers, you are really dreaming about sex organs.* Answer: *True, of course. Though some students, particularly during the period right before lunch, will try to argue that when you are dreaming about food, you are dreaming about food.*

LAW

Debate Question: *Should you be able to sue a person who gives you herpes?*

LIBRARY RESEARCH

What do Isaac Newton, Sigmund Freud, Alfred Hitchcock, and Michael Jackson have in common? Answer: *Allegedly, they were all celibate for a large part of their lives.*

The Student Reporter Asks:

What do you think would be the very best lesson you could give young adults of today? Please be specific.

"I'd hire as expensive a rock group as I could afford, but I'd also bring to class a TV monitor and a video camera. I'd set up the camera to record the performance, then I'd tell my students that they will either be allowed to stay and watch the performance or asked to leave depending on whether or not they conform to my Secret Rule. The rule would be: Keep your eye on the rock group, not on the TV monitor. That's about the best lesson I can think of for the young adults of today."

—A music teacher

When in Doubt, Maximize Gross Learning

Of course, the best teachers realize that sex is only one way to market learning. They know that a little (or a lot of) "grossness" works almost as well. However, a warning: Students of today's TV generation require visuals. You will not be able to generate many "yuks" from your class simply by stating that every bite of food we put in our mouths travels through thirty-three feet of digestive tract. You'll need to accompany this information with a huge full-color slide blowup of a squishy intestine. This slide will, of course, seem tame compared to the exquisitely graphic bad taste of last weekend's slasher movie, but after all, you don't want to pander.

However, remember that under their media-tough exteriors, kids of today are as vulnerable to being grossed out as kids ever were. This experiment will make the point:

The lesson for the day is that termites, with their chicken-like flavor and low calorie content, are good for us. Fry up a bunch of termites in front of the class, sample a few spoonfuls, and pass the plate around so the hearty may savor the delicacy. You will be as famous at your school as any teacher can be without breaking the law.

Employ Weird Questions

The weird question will wake up your class in a way that one more question about the provisions of the Sherman Anti-Trust Act will not. The characteristics of the weird question are:

1. *The question should have nothing to do with the topic under discussion. Think of it as the classroom equivalent of flicking the dial or cutting to a commercial.*
2. *The question should have an egalitarian quality. All students, regardless of ability, should have the same chance at a lucky guess.*
3. *The answer, if not the question, should induce most students to think "Huh?" However, a demonstrable show of interest may be too much to expect of any student who has turned fifteen.*

Here are some classroom-tested weird questions and answers:

Question: How many hairs are on the average adult male's face?
Answer: 15,500.
Question: Who is the most photographed person in history?
Answer: Probably, Elvis Presley.
Question: What is the most widely printed sentence in the English language?
Answer: Close before striking.
Question: The residents of which continent have the highest per capita I.Q.?
Answer: Antarctica. Remember all those research scientists.
Question: Quick. What do the first line and the last line of the

national anthem have in common?

Answer: They are questions.

As a Last Resort, Try the Absurd Statement

The absurd statement, a "fact" so patently false even the most credulous member of the class should recognize it as erroneous, should be employed only out of desperation. Save it for those moments when you confront a sea of catatonic stares that would outdo the expressions of the extras in *Invasion of the Body Snatchers*. If anyone is awake out there, someone should tell you you're wrong. Here are some classics of the genre:

- *Anacin works better if you swallow it with the arrows pointing down your throat.*
- *If you wear a hat inside the house you'll get a headache.*
- *If you stare at the back of someone's head long enough, he will turn around.*

If no one challenges these statements, call 911. The situation is beyond your control.

How to Be Relevant; or, Goodbye Basic Skills, Hello Critical Thinking

Pay attention. The educational times they are a-changin'—again.

For several years now FACTS and BASIC SKILLS have been in. But lately some very important Reports, Commissions, and Commissioned Reports have been asking, "Facts for what?" After all, out of 250 million people, how many can legitimately expect to get a shot at an appearance on "Jeopardy"?

The latest educational wisdom advocates a marriage between rigorous curriculum and practical thinking skills. The following sample questions will help you understand this concept, which is so old it is new.

Ask Questions That Encourage Careful Reading

Example: A close reading of the play we have been studying reveals one of the following characters to be *significantly* older than the other three.

a. King Lear.
b. His daughter Cordelia.
c. Cordelia's sister Goneril.
d. Goneril's sister Regan.

You may use your text.

Ask Questions That Demand Students Apply Theory to Practical Situations

Example: Discuss Darwin's theory of the survival of the fittest as it relates to the Los Angeles Raiders' defensive line.

Ask Questions That Require Students to Apply Knowledge of Survival Skills

Example: If Oliver Twist were around today, would he be eligible for SSI? What forms would he need to fill out? How many copies?

Ask Questions That Help Students Think Critically About Leisure and Recreation Activities

Example: Suppose, on the eve of Valley Forge, George Washington had been presented with a $5,000 money order from Eddie Bauer's. How could he best have spent this gift?

Ask Questions That Require Students to Solve Everyday Problems

Example: What could Holden Caulfield's parents have done to keep him from saying "goddamn" twice every other page?

Ask Questions That Require Students To Explore Logical Outcomes

Example: What grade do you think you will get in this class if the principal finds out what I said about him last week?

Ask Questions That Help Students Apply Learning to Job Situations

Example: You are working as an inspector at the office of the local Health Department when a woman comes in complaining that her uncle wants to leave her brother's body unburied for the carrion birds to peck away at. What code sections is the uncle violating?

Learn the Secrets of the Grading System

For years the grading in our schools has been bad-mouthed as arbitrary, capricious, and generally kinky. Nothing could be further from the truth. The fact is that the grading system operates according to twelve inexorable laws, revealed here for the first time.

LAW I. If a teacher is able to plot his test results on a perfect bell-shaped curve, either he or his students are cheating.

LAW II. Any student who will put up with the bulls——t necessary to get an A in a class deserves a C− on general principles.

LAW III. The best disguise for arbitrariness in grading is a number point system. The higher the numbers, the more effective the disguise.

LAW IV. The more obsessive a teacher's compulsion to give F's to those students who earn them, the more pressing her need for an unlisted phone number.

LAW V. During a teacher's career, the number of students who will report that their grades have been calculated too high will roughly equal the number of students from that teacher's classes who have won the Nobel Peace Prize.

LAW VI. At a faculty meeting, the more enthusiastic a teacher speaker's advocacy of the pass/fail grading system, the less likely she is to have experienced it.

LAW VII. There are two types of students who ask to do extra credit: those who do not need it and those who will not complete it.

LAW VIII. The semester that a teacher loses his grade book will be the semester the daughter of the president of the PTA earns a D+ in his class.

LAW IX. The more whimsical and cantankerous a teacher's grading system, the less the chance of her being replaced by an Apple II computer.

LAW X. Inside every C+ student is a B− student trying to get out.

LAW XI. All students are always on the borderline.

LAW XII. In any classroom, the percentage of B−, C−, and D− grades is directly proportional to the teacher's need to remain free of hassles with kids and parents.

 ## Ten Things to Think About While Grading Papers

A survey of several thousand teachers concludes that if none of the following ideas occurs to you as you correct papers, you are a very weird person.

1. Why is it that every time I count the papers in this pile, there are three more?
2. I know she didn't write this, but it's too bad to be plagiarized.
3. Whoops, I'd better write, "Melanie, please excuse the coffee ring."
4. Let's see—B−, C+; B−, C+. Maybe I'll just flip a coin.
5. Jeez, it's late; maybe I'll make this a check-off assignment.
6. So! This is where that Mastercard bill has been hiding.
7. If I put this chicken-scratching on the bottom of the pile, I'll only have to face it in the morning. However...
8. If I just write, "Good idea," "Interesting," and "I'd like to hear more about this," next to every third paragraph, I can get through this stack before "Hill Street Blues" starts.
9. Should I write, "Why not hand in the Cliff Notes and avoid the middleman?" or would that be unprofessional?
10. Maybe I'll just say tomorrow, "Sorry, kids, but the dog ate your homework—all of it."

How to Evade Your Students' Questions;
or,
"That Reminds Me of the Time I Met Cyndi Lauper..."

Maddening as you may find your students' inquisitiveness, remember you are paid to answer questions. For this reason, we provide here a little training exercise to help you prepare to deal with curious young minds. You have two minutes to give detailed, if evasive, answers to the following questions:

1. *Why don't they just collect all the presidents' bodies and dump them in one big memorial?*
2. *Why did God stoop so low as to make worms bisexual?*
3. *So then, who discovered Europe?*
4. *How did knights in armor go to the bathroom?*
5. *Does Mr. Hamtrack wear a wig?*
6. *How come they picked a puny place like Greenwich, England, to set all the clocks in the world by?*
7. *Are you gay?*
8. *What will happen if I eat this glue?*
9. *How do birds have sex?*
10. *Do you like being our teacher?*

Note: If you succeeded in evading each of the above questions, you should consider leaving education

and taking a job as public information person for some nuclear waste dump.

Stop Feeling Guilty About All Those Papers You Haven't Corrected!

Put down that red pen! Experts now tell us you can inhibit a child's love of learning AND GET SUED if you bleed sarcasm all over her homework assignments. In other words, you had better keep your frustration concerning wildly inaccurate percentages (i.e., "330 percent of the trains arrived at the station on time") to yourself if you want to avoid appearances in psychiatrists' offices AND COURTROOMS.

Now, this may not be easy if you have become mildly addicted to venting your spleen over student illiteracies.

But, if you are truly sincere, you can break the habit of lashing out in red ink.

How?

By ceasing to find fault with your students' homework assignments.

You say it's impossible? You say the very sight of a dangling participle makes you reach for a pen? Well, fear not—help is on the way.

How to Stop Correcting Papers Without Feeling Guilty

1. *Lock yourself in a room with no red pencils or pens.*

2. *Read the following student essay over and over and over.*

3. *On the day when this essay begins to sound like the work of*

Jane Austen, you are clean. YOU WILL NEVER HAVE TO CORRECT A PAPER AGAIN!

Debbi Dunn
English, Period 4

What I did on My Summer Vacation

About all I did on my summer vacation was go to Disneyland because of my uncle and ant who like to do boring things when they come to visit so we did.

I did not mind going too much because of Michael Jackson who I heard likes to go and ride on Pirates of the Carribean which is my favorite ride so I thought it might not be too boring because I would see him even though I didn't.

When we got to P. of the C. there was numerous crowds stretching my eyeballs as far as they could see.

My cousins and parents began taking pictures of ourselves and my uncle was having fun at his age. While you stand there I like the fictional characters who come around playing with you. Minnie Mouse didn't shake my hand but almost every child and quite a few adults walk around with her ears on there heads.

Disneyland is mostly getting into boxcars and going through things so when we got inside of P. of the C. I noticed it was a gigantic place of its own and you saw sailors who chase women until along the way there were wars with cannonballs that almost hit me in the head.

In conclusion, Disneyland is pretty boring unless you are the type of person who likes to take trips like everyone else.

6

Social Studies; or, What Teachers Do When They Aren't Teaching, Grading, Planning, Coaching, Supervising, Attending Meetings, or Working Second Jobs

One of the best ways to anger a teacher is to say, "Gosh, I envy you for all that free time you have." The truth is, teachers spend only a fraction of their working hours in their classrooms. Yes, they do get off "work" at 3:30 or so, but then it's off to bus duty, and from there to the gymnasium, where they get to spend the twilight hours coaching would-be gymnasts, basketball players, and cheerleaders. And, when that's finished, you can bet the teacher has a P.T.A. meeting to attend, papers to grade, and lessons to plan.

What about those two-week vacations for Christmas or Chanukah? The typical teacher spends at least twelve of those fourteen days lying in bed, staring at the ceiling, and mumbling something like, "Row three, we're still waiting for you to quiet down."

Then there is summer vacation. That's when the average teacher gets to choose whether he or she would like to (a) teach summer school, (b) drive a taxicab, (c) waitress, or (d) collect food stamps.

Of course, even the most harried teacher makes frantic attempts to have *some* kind of social life. Some teachers even manage to get married and have children. No one has ever quite figured out how that happens: "You mean she married him even after she found out he's a teacher?" I hear they're both teachers—do you think the kids know they're adopted yet?" "I hear she absolutely promised she'd quit teaching fourth grade and find a less nerve-wracking job—like go into brain surgery or something."

To assist teachers in making the most of their free time, we sought out all the teachers across the country who have managed to combine teaching with an exciting social life. All three of them consented to be interviewed. Our findings are reported in this chapter.

Teachers and Cocktail Parties

Unfortunately, Holden Caulfield was speaking for millions when he said, "You don't have to think too hard to talk to a teacher." However, as "hard thinking" is not exactly a characteristic of cocktail-party chatter, you might expect your profession would not prove a liability on the wine and Brie circuit. Wrong. When your fellow partygoers find out you are a teacher, they often decide they would rather communicate with the *hors d'oeuvre* tray. It's as if they're afraid you are going to assign homework. As you cannot report these defectors to the dean for leaving before the bell, you are going to have to work out some other strategies to hold their attention. Consider these principles:

1. *Realize that people feel uncomfortable with a teacher because they do not know what to say.* When we meet a plumber at a party we say, "My toilet is making weird noises in the night. What could it be?" or "I hear you guys make more an hour than doctors." But no one is going to say to a teacher, "I've been looking for someone who can help me get rid of my dangling modifiers." And most people are too polite to mention your salary.

2. *Do not try to impress non-teachers with what a special teacher you are.* Some teachers make it known right off that they are not your generic-brand educator. They say, "I teach gifted," or "I get a period off for curriculum." For all the status this will give them with the general populace, they may as well be bragging about their collection of flip-top can lids.

3. *Be an expert on something other than teaching.* It does not make much difference what it is—the filmography of Donald Duck or the best way to win at whist—anything at all that says, "I know more about the world than just the difference between phonics and look-say."

As you keep these conversational principles in mind, however, you'll need to learn how to cope with the following:

How to Cope with Sex Talk

Since the average teacher is assumed to have the sex drive of an

octogenarian eunuch, you are not going to get many propositions. The closest thing to a sexual offer you are likely to hear will be: "You don't look like a teacher," in which case respond, "Your place or mine?"

How to Cope with "My Kid" Talk

The perpetrator of "My Kid" talk thinks that because you teach kids

so he never got any feedback as to what he was doing wrong. Anyway, he took it hard, spiked his hair, and spent hours and hours in his room gorging on Fritos. But then we found some wonderful, sensitive people at La Crème Academy who understood what a bright, creative, kid Brad really is. And the good news is Brad just made the Dean's List after his first year at Dartmouth. No thanks, unfortunately, to the public-school system."

You should say: "I hand back homework."

How to Cope with Talk about the Subject on Which You're Supposedly an Expert

Occasionally someone at a party will ask you about the subject matter you teach. He will be the type who studies Trivial Pursuit cards in his bathroom, and he will almost always be quite drunk.

He will say: "You teach history? Say, you might be able to settle a little argument my wife and I are having: What year was it Marco Polo sailed to Cathay?"

You should say: "It was either 1275 or 7512."

How to Cope with "I-Am-Not-Like-You" Talk

you want to hear about *her* kid. The "My Kid" monologue goes like this: "We became very concerned about Brad after his ninth-grade teacher gave him a D–. She was the kind who *never* handed back homework,

Often at a party you find yourself standing in the center of the room like some extraterrestrial while the other guests compete with one another to distance themselves from

91

you, bombarding you with "I-Am-Not-Like-You" talk:

"Oh, I'd never have the patience to be a teach—"

You should say: "Excuse me, I just have to grab another shrimp canapé before they're all gone."

"I was never good at (whatever you teach—it could be remedial tiddlywinks)."

You should say: "That's a shame. But now we have special programs for the mentally disadvantaged."

"I'd better watch my grammar."

You should say: "You do that while I watch that hunk over by the wet bar."

How to Cope with Strike Talk

A teachers' strike may play hell with your pocketbook, but it is great for your social life. When you put down your Dolch cards and pick up your picket placard, you join the real world of wages, hours, and working conditions. Now, you are into avarice: something people understand.

As a striking teacher you will be a star attraction: "Step right this way, ladies and gentlemen. See the Idealist turned Money Grubber."

Everyone at the cocktail party will leer and want to know how much money you are losing.

When you answer, exaggerate; throw in an extra fifty dollars or so a day. But if you are enjoying all this attention, do not under any circumstances say: "I am doing this for the kids."

If you commit this *faux pas*, you will be summarily banished from center stage, and made to rejoin the company of Trotskyite librarians, unemployed ex-VISTA workers, and other fuzzyheads who have never met a payroll.

How to Cope with School-Reform Talk

Most school-reform talk you'll hear proposes little nostrums for change that are so vague and chimerical they could have originated with a presidential commission.

The school reformer says: "I'm all for higher salaries, but first we need to get the deadwood out of the schools."

You should say: "Some of my best friends are coniferous."

How to Cope with "You-Must-Be-Very-Strange" Talk

This talk often starts as gentle probing: "So, you're a teacher. Do you like it?"

To this you may answer "Yes," but be prepared for the reaction. No one wants to believe that an adult actually enjoys being around eight-year-olds. Sometimes the questions will turn nasty. "How can you do it?" they will ask, as if you were spending your life constructing a doomsday machine in your garage. This time stand tall and answer:

"I don't really feel like apologizing for doing important work."

Note: There are many jokes in this book, but this is not one of them.

The Teacher's Sex Life

Sex and schools go together like *pâté de foie gras* and your local 7-Eleven. Rumors persist of places less sexy than the average American school: An office of the Nuclear Regulatory Commission in Omaha, Nebraska, is said to be in the running. In general, however, the school system is the institutional saltpeter of our society. Each day we collect millions of hot-blooded adolescents and dump them into a cold shower of a building: pea-green walls, *cinéma vérité* acoustics, bells, buzzers—all calculated to annihilate the sexual appetite of the horniest teenager.

As a teacher, what is your role in this conspiracy? You are to be out there on patrol just in case some pubescent pair—against all odds—manage to get their tongues in the general vicinity of each other's mouths. You are expected to be on the spot, ready to bellow, "Do you know where that kind of thing leads?" The couple, of course, hopes it will lead to the abandoned gardener's shack behind the football bleachers, but they are also smart enough to know you'll do what you can to prevent this maneuver.

However, just the fact that you as a teacher must assume the responsibilities of an academic vice cop does not mean you should not, at the same time, emit a sexual aura all your own. The stereotype of the chaste schoolmarm went out with the days when teachers were fired for hanging around ice cream parlors after dark.

Now, in our "Sex Is God" era, it is OK to let a little of your libido show.

This does not mean, of course, that you should go so far as to actually copulate after 9:30 on a school night. Your first responsibility, after all, is to get the spelling tests back on time. Abandon yourself to carefree debauchery, and your lesson plans are going to get pretty raggedy. You aren't likely to be able to summon up much enthusiasm for a discussion of the Roosevelt Corollary to the Monroe Doctrine if you have been out until 3:30 A.M. thrashing around at Plato's Retreat.

But at the same time, it is quite acceptable to give the impression around school that you are respectably licentious. Your colleagues, many of whose last depraved act was reading a pirated copy of *Lady Chatterley's Lover* in 1953, will admire your appearance of restrained dissipation. With a little planning, you can become a legend—sort of an Errol Flynn with a roll book or a Marilyn Monroe with bus duty.

Here are five ways to improve your sexual image around school:
1. Ask a friend to call the office and leave a message, saying he is from the Acme Glass Company. He should ask whether you want clear, or blue-tinted glass on the mirror the workers are installing on your ceiling.
2. Mail to yourself, at school, plain brown envelopes containing objects that are hard, long, and blunt, or soft and rubbery.

3. Make up dirty answers to multiple-choice questions.

Examples:

1. *Major changes in the American industrial system have been brought about by*
   a. *automation.*
   b. *autobiography.*
   c. *autocrats.*
   d. *autoeroticism.*

2. *Napoleon Bonaparte was a French*
   a. *writer.*
   b. *chef.*
   c. *emperor.*
   d. *tickler.*

4. Regularly arrive at school one minute before starting time, breathless and slightly disheveled. Do this even on those mornings when you have been up since 5:00 A.M. grading maps of Latin America, and you will develop a reputation that would make Alex Comfort jealous.

5. Sprinkle your lunchtime conversation with figures of speech that allude to sexual practices: "This new method of recording absences they're laying on us is about as uncomplicated as the Chinese Basket Trick" or, "The day the Dean of Girls shows a little compassion will be the same day she demonstrates the Golden Shower Technique at an all-school assembly."

Note: If you are a bit fuzzy on the details of these practices, don't worry: *you are speaking to teachers.* Everyone will laugh knowingly; they will not admit they do not know what you are talking about.

However, while it is exhilarating to bring your sex life (however fanciful) to school, you must never bring school to your sex life. Schoolteaching is not exactly up there with airline piloting as one of the aphrodisiac professions. You are about as likely to turn on a potential sex partner with "I teach eighth grade" as you are with a button that reads, "I Have Herpes and I'm Proud."

But consider this: Neither law nor custom mandates that you explain to the body on the next barstool what you do for a living. Dope dealers, escaped cons, very rich people, and plenty of others who get a lot more action than your average schoolteacher remain closemouthed about their lives. So, you see, you are really not required to babble on about your Thanksgiving bulletin-board display. Look in any "relationship" book and you will read how you can excite the object of your lust beyond endurance if you will just shut up and pretend to listen while the other talks about himself or herself.

However, this said, you will need to prepare for the day—at about the time your new friend moves a toothbrush into your bathroom—when you will no longer be able to keep your secret. When that day arrives, you will need to come up with a reason you hang around a school all day long. Some suggestions:

- *You are a narc about to bust an international teenybopper cocaine ring.*
- *You are posing as a teacher while researching a high school exposé that Jackie O. assures you will be a six-figure best*

seller—plus film, miniseries, and tee-shirt rights.

• *You are scouting locations for Porky's IV.*

Teachers in relationships are particularly burdened by their habit of evaluating all they survey. Thus, you need to understand that grading students in social-studies class is one thing, but grading lovers in bed is an entirely different matter. In the classroom, the best teachers assign candid marks—A to F—based on performance. That won't work in bed. The 1980s, the New Age of Romance, allows only three acceptable grades: A, A+, and Incomplete. The A and A+ verdicts must be assigned in a breathless whisper, as in "Whooo, that was straight A." The incomplete performance, of course, must not actually be labeled Incomplete. Better to say, "We'll try again later." Or, if more appropriate: "Hey there, you may be finished, but I'm not."

 ## Sex and Teachers: Five No-Nos

1. When you write a note to your lover cataloguing all the exotic and unspeakable acts the two of you will perform on each other this weekend, DO NOT USE RED PENCIL.

2. If your lover brings over a copy of Masters and Johnson or *The Joy of Sex*, do not grade him down if his book isn't covered.

3. If your lover invites you to meet for a "nooner," better cancel the whole thing before you admit that the only time you have is between 12:13 and 1:02, and then only if you can get off cafeteria duty.

4. If, during sex, your lover encourages you to speak of your fantasies, it's OK to talk about doing it on a ski lift or with Louis XIV, but stay away from the weird stuff like your dreams of lower class size or a classroom clock that works.

5. When your lover expresses an interest in having sex, do not, under any circumstances, say, "You forgot to use the magic word."

What Teachers Know That Most People Do Not Know

There are professional, college-educated people out there who are required to eat lunch at 10:45 in the morning.

It is not uncommon for someone in our society to sit for 14,000 hours in a classroom and still not know for sure what a sentence is.

Any adult who can suggest an activity that a fourteen-year-old does not find boring probably belongs in jail.

The sound of a Scantron machine correcting multiple-choice tests comes very close to the sound of Walter Mitty's "ta-pocketa-pocketa."

In America, it is possible to go to work and come home for days in a row—without ever once speaking to an adult.

Extra credit is a shuck.

Bloom's Taxonomy is not a place on Hester Street that stuffs animals.

In a school, it is the "floater" teacher who is most likely to drown.

Most every day, someplace in America, at about 3:50 P.M., a group of people, many with master's degrees, engage in sometimes rancorous debate on questions such as, "Is it OK to use a signature stamp when making out report cards?"

What Teachers Don't Do

This book is intended to define and describe the Teacherly Life, but at the same time, the author recognizes that there are thousands of you out there who understand that life well enough and want desperately to break out of the stereotype. It is for you that the following list is provided. Do any of these things and you will establish yourself as an educational flasher.

Teachers Don't:

- *ask a car dealer if there will be a discount for buying two BMWs at the same time*
- *stay up all night playing Space Invaders at 7-Eleven*
- *work hard to achieve a Mr. T. Look*
- *open Swiss bank accounts*
- *affix bumper stickers that read, "I ♥ Ludes"*
- *speculate in pork bellies as a hedge against inflation*
- *serve pork bellies for dinner*
- *thank Paine Webber*
- *send back a steak at any restaurant tonier than the Sizzler*
- *have their homes featured in* Architectural Digest.

- *fire someone*
- *take a job because of "generous perks"—whatever they are*
- *mean it when they say, "Your guess is as good as mine"*
- *ask a fashion consultant about organizing a Power Wardrobe*
- *throw rice at a performance of* The Rocky Horror Picture Show
- *call in sick to attend a demolition derby*
- *appear as guests on the "Donahue Show"*

7

Your Students: Wild in the Streets...

How Well Do You Know Your Students? A Picture Quiz

See if you can match the following students' names and biographies with their pictures. Just fill in the letter of the photograph that best suits each student's personality, and then check your prowess at the bottom of the following page:

1. Stephanie "Steph" Henderson wants to be co-captain of the cheerleading squad, president of Student Council, and "a nice person who is friendly even to unpopular kids." _____

2. How did Stanley "the Trans Am is a fine machine" Simkus manage to pass each and every one of his classes this year in spite of the fact that the only time his teachers ever saw him was after school, when Stanley fixed their cars free of charge? _____

3. Three years ago, Ms. Dylan-Baez Smith was ringleader of the underground group that "liberated" Hexter, her sixth-grade class's pet hamster. A vegetarian, Dylan-Baez subsists on a diet of herbal cigarettes and Milk Duds. _____

4. Although his I.Q. puts him in the genius range, Harvey Sherman has never earned more than a C in his life. What can be done with a boy who believes the world's greatest historical figure is Conan the Barbarian? _____

5. Andrea "I would have been in class yesterday except I got a run in my pantyhose" Atwood is willing to carry her books home from school as long as they are color coordinated. Look for Andrea in the girls' bathroom, where rumor has it she has become a millionaire at the age of fifteen by piercing ears for five dollars a lobe. _____

6. Although Doug Buchanan is believed to be deaf, he isn't: It's just that he usually forgets to remove the cotton that his mother forces him to wear in his ears when he plays his electric guitar. _____

7. There are days when Cordelia Siegel wonders if her chemistry teacher would leave his wife for someone who has never scored lower than a 96 on a lab test. _____

(. . . and in Your Classroom, Too)

Answer Key: (1)A; (2)D; (3)G; (4)B; (5)E; (6)F; (7)C.

What Students Know That Teachers Will Never Know

Come on, admit it. You can't really distinguish between Punk and New Wave. Does it tell you something that none of your students suffer from the same confusion? Let's take a moment out here to recognize that while we find ourselves appalled and depressed that not one student in ten knows anything about the Bosporus Straits, we teachers also draw a blank once in a while. Here, then, is a list of things your students know that you do not know.

You should find it cleansing, even humbling:

Students know that one-half piece of Hubba Bubba is enough to chew at one time. A whole piece will give them away.

★   ★   ★

Students know who in your class wears contact lenses.

★   ★   ★

Students know that "Beat It" is a golden oldie.

★   ★   ★

Students know how many weeks of allowance it takes to save up for a pair of black leather pants.

★ ★ ★

Students know that driving a car, even in bumper-to-bumper traffic on a ninety-seven-degree day with the air conditioner on the blink, is the ultimate status symbol.

★ ★ ★

Students know there has not yet been a *Rocky V*—it only seems that way to you.

★ ★ ★

Students know how long it takes to get downtown on a bus.

★ ★ ★

Students know the exact date of the next school holiday. (They do not know its significance.)

★ ★ ★

Students know geometry does not necessarily build character.

★ ★ ★

Students know why they giggle when you make hip references to *Saturday Night Fever* and even, God forbid, the Beach Boys.

★ ★ ★

Students know that John Taylor sleeps naked.

★ ★ ★

Students know a person can stay alive for several days—and even feel kinda sexy—on a diet of M & M's and Diet Pepsi.

★ ★ ★

Students know that if Rob Lowe, Tommy Howell, or Ralph Macchio were to walk into your classroom at this very moment, nothing would ever be quite the same again.

★ ★ ★

Students know the cough code for sending signals during a true/false test.

★ ★ ★

Students know you forgot to zip up the back of your dress.

★ ★ ★

Students know which video arcade gives the most tokens for a dollar.

★ ★ ★

Students know the true meaning of the word "grody" as only one who has been in the girls' bathroom could.

★ ★ ★

Students know that if the topping from a pizza falls on a girl's lap at the exact moment her eyes make contact with those of the mega-gorgeous captain of the football team, her life (for all practical purposes) has ended.

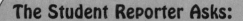

The Student Reporter Asks:

If you were going to get hit by a car and drop dead tomorrow, what would you do today in school that would be different since you would be dead tomorrow?

"If this were my last day of life (and I had to spend it in school), I would get out of my classroom and go through the day with one of my kids. This is a big building and sometimes I forget it was not constructed solely to instruct kids in the fine points of quadratic equations. Once in a while, I'll be walking around the campus and I'll hear a kid I've had in math class say something in French, or see her running what looks like a fast 440 in P.E. and I'll say to myself, "Is this the same girl who can't get binomials straight?" I'd like to leave my life thinking I helped in a process that was more important than what went on in my classroom, or in any teacher's classroom. I say I'd like to do this on my last day in school (and on Earth), but I guess I should have done it the very first day I started teaching here."

—A math teacher

If Teachers Were Mind Readers

As far as your students are concerned, school is a prison, you are a warden, and they are prisoners. And why shouldn't they feel this way? Do *they* choose to be students? Do *they* get paid to come to school?

Those smug teachers who get to teach honors classes like to believe that *their* students are different. *Their* students want to *learn*; *their* students *like them*; *their* students *behave* and don't take *their* money out of *their* purses. That's right: *Their* students are model prisoners.

As prisoners, students have learned how to "do time": They keep their eyes open, their backs straight, and their minds on "getting sprung" seven minutes to recess, three years to graduation.

Your students are also thinking:

105

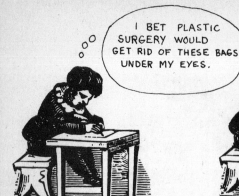

106

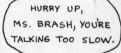

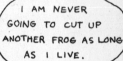

Kidspeak: Questions and Excuses

Check the following list. If you have heard any of the following more than 7,500 times, you may qualify for a disability pension.

Questions

You a sub?
Where do I sit?
Can I do extra credit?
How come we never get movies in this class?
Is it OK to use pencil?
How many words is this supposed to be?
Why do we have to do this?
Do we have to take notes?
Does spelling count?
How come there are no good-looking girls in this class?
How we supposed to answer this?
Can I print?
Are we doing anything today?

Excuses

Somebody stole it out of my locker.
Ms. Hacksham used to let us.
I brung the wrong book.
I can't read your writing.
I got eyestrain.
I .thought you said the odd-numbered problems.
We never had this.
I got a PERMANENT pass.
You didn't say we had to bring . . .
I didn't do nothing.
You're the only teacher who makes us . . .
He started it.

I lost my glasses.
SAVED BY THE BELL!

What Your Students Want to Know That You Can't Teach

 How to live on chocolate alone.

 How to keep food out of braces.

 How to look older.

 How to get a rock group that has never been out of the garage onto MTV.

 How to develop a repertoire of Totally Tasteless Jokes no one else has heard.

How to avoid being "molded" several times a week.

How Creative Are Your Students?

You may have noticed that, on those days when you are not present, your students are often at their most creative. Pranks played on substitutes provide a classic format for student imagination.

Leave the following form letter for your substitute to use. Upon your return, you will be able to judge just how inventive your charges were when left to their own devices. We include a brief analysis of each prank.

Dear Substitute,

Please indicate which, if any, of the following methods my students used today to drive you crazy:

Wads of spit-filled paper thrown at the ceiling when you are not looking.

Consider this a low-level prank, an act of individual terrorism that requires no group planning. No points are awarded if (a) the student is caught in the act of salivating on the binder paper, (b) the wad fails to adhere to the ceiling, or (c) the student is caught in the act of throwing the wad. So far, no student has *ever* been caught throwing the wad.

All pencils dropped at exactly 10:30.

This prank, which occurs regularly in all fifty states, Guam, and American Samoa, is more an exercise in teamwork than in creativity. The experienced substitute is likely to foil this one in the preparation stage by intercepting a note. The pencil ploy is hardest to thwart, however, with a class of eighth-graders whose perpetual squirminess serves as a perfect cover for all sorts of covert activity.

Chalk placed in the ribs of a blackboard eraser.

Again, this prank is so common it cannot be given points for originality. However, the caper does suggest a kind of kamikaze desperation. It is, after all, the student as well as the teacher who will be assaulted by the harrowing screech of the chalk when it connects with the board. Only a feverish compulsion to avoid the even-numbered problems would inspire such a rash act.

Vicks Vaporub smeared underneath the eyes of all students to induce tears.

This less common prank demands considerable skill. Imagine the degree of subterfuge required to pass a jar of ointment among thirty students right under the eyes of the teacher. In evaluating this activity consider: (a) Is the varsity linebacker willing to put aside his image and apply this crud for the good of the group? (b) When does the crying occur? Students should get high points for ironic juxtapositions. An inspired dramatic reading from *Cyrano de Bergerac* might be expected to induce a few tears, but a good cry when a substitute announces, "I'm going to give you some time off to socialize quietly"—now that's pure Dada.

Smiling students in one corner of the room, frowns everywhere else.

We have here high-level and uncommon stuff. The purpose of the prank is to attract your total attention, and even your body, to that little nucleus of good cheer in the corner. From my point of view, this is the ideal student caper. The kids have their fun, and as you do not know you are being made to look foolish, you can save your ego. The whole episode takes on the quality of one of those little experiments *Psychology Today* would be pleased to describe in print.

Sincerely,

Your name here

A Sampling of Your Students' Finest Prose

Some teachers, not otherwise enthralled by their jobs, enjoy going to work each day just because they know they will be able to add to their collection of student illiteracies. Over the years they develop a connoisseur's selection of historical ignorance, primitive style, logical abuse, and grammatical *faux pas*. These teachers insist that there is enormous pleasure to be had in their hobby.

Below are unexpurgated samples of student writing so you can get started on your own collection:

Sometimes lady writers were so prejudiced against that they had to call themselves by names like George even though they probably weren't gay.

In the scene with Bottom and the other workmen, Shakespeare shows one of the best senses of humor anyone could ever hope to meet.

Like all normal teenage boys I am interested in sex, but I think I am too young to appreciate girls practicing to do things on carrots like they did in Fast Times At Ridgemont High.

In some of the olden love stories like Wuthering Heights the characters are trying to show love toward each other, but it was hard for authors in those days because of the words they could not use to describe.

So much that happens in the world today is not fit for human eye sockets or ears.

In the past, I have never looked forward to reading an Edgar Allen Poe story with regret, and "The Pit and the Pendulum" is no exception.

After a while Hitler gave Germany a pretty bad name.

I think most kids would agree that the best way to read books is to see them in the movies.

In the ball scene Romeo manages to put a few moves on Juliet.

Right now I would have to say my life reeks with JOY!!

I know how Echo felt about Narcissus because even today if you want to go out with a guy who doesn't pay any attention to you you can get confused and overwhelming and just want to give up.

The pressure from the Watergate commotion affected President Nixon in his head, but later he wrote a book.

At the time of the Black Plague the lifestyle of many people was badly degraded.

The story about how Georg Washington never told a lie is not true, but it is not exactly a lie of the kind George Washington sometimes told.

The Joads did not realize that a part of Grandpa died when the family forced him to go to California instead of starving peacefully on the land.

Joan of Arcs gross death symbolized that she couldn't cope with many of the bad parts of her society.

In this story, the availability of Moby Dick becomes unattainable.

In quite a few pages of *Tale of Two Cities*, incidents of violence lashed out at people in the story.

According to the author of this book, traveling in Europe is where Mr. and Mrs. Fitzgearld spent their vacations. It says that both Mr. and Mrs. Fitzgearld drank a lot, but in my opinion, he wrote a good book anyway.

Our neighbor was put in the paper as a human interest story, but there were too many lies so he quit his subscription.

In this class I have learened that a good reference book is supposed to develop a non-biased attitude toward the subject in graphic detail.

So many people like Joan Collins on TV that rave reviews concerning the uncontrollable passion she possesses flood her constantly.

In the law of supply and demand, everybody buys something like potatoes all at once, but sooner or later people get nauseated and the production gets smaller for a while.

In the encyclopedia it said that ice cream and royalty were associated in the past. They were made from mixing snow and fruit juices.

Other examples of bad horror movies for children are things such as deformed people killing other people with strange quirks, people living in asylums and later killing themselves, and aliens which eat human flesh, the list goes on.

Oedipus's tragic flaw shines like the sun in this play but he was a hero so people didn't feel too sorry for him.

Othello has attained a high rank even though in his younger years he presented barbaric ways. When he sees the truth about Desdemona from gullibility he plunges back into barbarism.

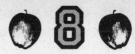

An Inside Look at Principals, Parents, and School-Board Members; or, Beware These Hazardous Wastes

Have you ever had one of those nightmares in which a parent takes you to court? There you sit, squirming, as the prosecuting attorney (your principal) drones on and on: "March third, the defendant threw away a set of homework papers, ungraded. April sixteenth, the accused said the word *damn* when she accidentally stapled her finger into one of the macraméd milk cartons her third-graders were making in art class; May twelfth, this very same teacher misspelled the word *embarrass* in three-inch-high letters on her chalkboard..." You turn your eyes toward the jury, hoping to see a friendly face, only to discover that— horror of horrors—the jury is en-tirely made up of members of the School Board.

Now, such a nightmare may be an expression of irrational fears. But remember what they say: Just because you are paranoid does not mean no one is out to get you.

Know Your School Board

As pecking orders go, teachers are pretty close to the bottom. They have, however, found their whipping boys: the members of the School Board—a class of individuals of such limited vision that they

113

would rather spend their evenings debating bids to patch the roof over the school's gym than watching "Dynasty" on TV. Now, while we do not wish to discourage the exercise of a little healthy contempt, we believe teachers ought to take a close look at the objects of their ridicule. Get to know those people who think you can survive on $13,500 a year, for they are the ones who decide who gets the pink slip—and we aren't referring to lingerie.

The Public Servant
In addition to serving on the School Board, this man is on the boards of United Way, the Boy Scouts, the Health Week Committee, the Heart Association, two local hospitals, and the zoo. In other words, he'll use any excuse to get out of the house.

The Politician
He is the one who shows up to cut the ribbon on the remodeled girls' lavatory. He is also the one who speaks at the Lion's Club about "dynamic educational programs to meet the challenge of tomorrow"—without raising taxes, of course.

The Den Mother
This woman has succeeded in parlaying her chairmanship of the bake-sale phone tree into a political machine that "puts kids first"—and teachers last.

The Traditionalist
This woman's main contribution to meetings is questions that begin with, "Why is it students no longer...?" Thus: "Why is it students no longer study Latin...parse sentences...memorize poems?" Sometimes, when the Assistant Superintendent gets peevish, he insists he is going to tell her why, but the Traditionalist is in frail health, and the Assistant Superintendent is not a cruel man.

The Accountant
This man takes a sharp pencil to any school programs smacking of waste, though he seems to have overlooked the $5,000 cost of the Superintendent's junket to the Bahamas to attend a seminar on "Rolfing and Rapping for Public Managers."

The Reformer
Board members went along with her demands that Malcolm X's birthday and Susan B. Anthony's birthday be declared school holidays but drew the line at her plan to close down the schools for a week so that students might honor the anniversary of the Tet offensive.

The Yuppie

Approach with care any parent who calls you by your first name. She's the type who considers your colleague—who insists that kids color between the lines—just one step above a child molester. She nods approvingly when you say "Piagetian," and believes her son needs "space" to "do his own thing," as long as he does whatever is necessary to get into Harvard Law School. If the kid doesn't make it, whose fault is it?
One guess.

The Gossip

Look out for the Rona Barrett of your school district. She'll tell you about those panties found in the Superintendent's office after the last Board of Education meeting, and the seven grammatical errors in the letter from the Back-to-Basics legislator. She gathers her dirt in the name of school reform. In particular, her reform is focused on getting a certain student's American history grade raised upward from a D to something a respectable college might accept. You say you can't do this? Well, about that attractive man seen leaving your apartment at four in the morning in October of 1963...

The Part-Time Parent

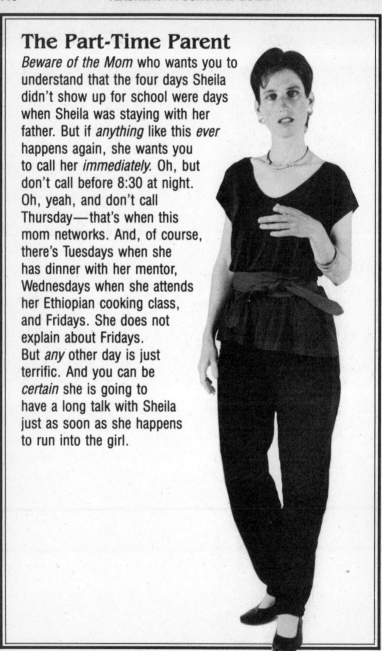

Beware of the Mom who wants you to understand that the four days Sheila didn't show up for school were days when Sheila was staying with her father. But if *anything* like this *ever* happens again, she wants you to call her *immediately.* Oh, but don't call before 8:30 at night. Oh, yeah, and don't call Thursday—that's when this mom networks. And, of course, there's Tuesdays when she has dinner with her mentor, Wednesdays when she attends her Ethiopian cooking class, and Fridays. She does not explain about Fridays. But *any* other day is just terrific. And you can be *certain* she is going to have a long talk with Sheila just as soon as she happens to run into the girl.

The Reactionary

Keep your back to the wall when talking with the parent who wears an expression that makes you wonder if maybe you should have changed your socks. This is the dad who would like to ask you if you're a communist. Instead, he asks how many race riots those nine black students in the school have started so far.

The Invisible Mom

Be wary of the parent you have never
seen. She is not there when you phone;
she is not there when you send a
letter; she is not there when you
pin notes on her child begging
her to show up at Parents' Night.
But, make no mistake about it,
she *will* be there in the
courtroom one day when
it comes time to sue
you because her kid
can't read.

The Parent–Teacher Conference

Since parents and teachers represent two distinct species of humanity, we can expect that the Parent–Teacher Conference will be given over to a mutual sniffing out: talking past each other, exchanging guarded euphemisms. And that's how it should be, for if parents and teachers were ever to speak their minds freely, there probably wouldn't be many parents and teachers left on this planet.

Here, then, is a guide to what parents and teachers should and should not say:

★★

Teacher Talk   Parent Talk

★★

Teacher Says: Kevin is not performing up to his potential . . .
Teacher Does Not Say: . . . But of course he's too young for San Quentin anyway.

Parents Says: You're very young, aren't you?
Parent Does Not Say: Just you TRY to give me a single word of advice about how to raise my kid.

★   ★   ★

Teacher Says: Kevin tends to act out.
Teacher Does Not Say: When this kid is on a rampage he will latch onto anything that can be hurled, punctured, or torn apart. How can you live with this holy terror?

Parent Says: Kevin's fourth grade was a total loss.
Parent Does Not Say: And the way things are going with you, I'm not holding out much hope for the fifth grade, either.

★ ★ ★

Teacher Says: Kevin does not seem to be a visual learner.
Teacher Does Not Say: This kid can't read.

Parents Says: What can we do to help?
Parent Does Not Say: We'll do just about anything except sit down with the kid for five minutes a night and help him with his schoolwork.

★ ★ ★

Teacher Says: Kevin needs just a little more self-discipline.
Teacher Does Not Say: What we have here is a prime candidate for lead singer in the Sex Pistols.

Parents Says: I don't have this problem at home.
Parent Does Not Say: And if you believe that one, I've got this bridge I'd like to sell you.

★ ★ ★

Teacher Says: I have another appointment at four, and it's five minutes to four now.
Teacher Does Not Say: If I hear one more word about how your ex-husband screwed up this kid, I'll scream.

Parents Says: You know, it's very difficult to raise a boy without a father there to help.
Parent Does Not Say: And, of course, my never being home probably doesn't help the kid much, either.

★ ★ ★

Teacher Says: Well, it's been a pleasure getting to know you.
Teacher Does Not Say: God, no wonder the kid is so screwed up.

Parents Says: I'm so glad I've been able to meet Kevin's teacher.
Parent Does Not Say: God, no wonder the kid is so screwed up.

Principals You Have Known, if Not Loved... or Even Liked Much

Toward the middle of each school day, the French teacher, the chemistry teacher, and the driver's education instructor climb out of their cubbyholes and head for the lunchroom, where they exchange pleasantries about the weather and the headlines in the newspaper, then get down to the important subject of the day: the latest gossip about the principal. If the principal did not exist, teachers would have to invent him. He serves as a unifier for every faculty—particularly when he is divisive. It is OK to tell nasty stories about him because he makes more money than you do and has a carpet in his office. Principal-watching is edging out sleeping past dawn on weekends as a major teacher hobby. That's why you are not likely to be meeting for the first time the men and women described on these pages:

Mr. Bybook

Background: As a beginning typing teacher he went right to work acquiring the tools of the principal's trade. He became well known as the youngest (perhaps the only) person ever to understand the formula for allocation of pupil–teacher contact hours. Ask him about it if you have four hours to spare and uncontrollable masochistic tendencies.

Educational Philosophy: To paraphrase—"If nothing changes, everything will get better." Each year, for instance, Backwater Middle School adds to its record of consecutive years in which no student has been injured on a field trip. "Now what would happen to this record if all of a sudden we allowed field trips?" Mr. Bybook asks.

Administrative Style: Keeps his door open, but not his mind. You are welcome to drop by anytime, and let him tell you what a fool you are.

Proudest Accomplishment: Demonstrating at last years' Back-to-School Week Open House that it is possible for the bulletin boards in *every* classroom to be arranged so pictures are exactly thirteen inches apart, the distance prescribed by *Administrative Bulletin 123: Displays in the Middle-School Classroom.*

Favorite Expression: "No."

Prize Possession: Leatherbound copy of *Administrative Bulletin 123: Displays in the Middle-School Classroom.*

Ms. Gowflow

Background: Ten years ago she was facilitating interdisciplinary finger-painting projects in a geodesic dome as head teacher at the Synergy Alternative Middle School. She got back into consonant blends just in time.

Educational Philosophy: 1975— "Personhood is where it's at." 1985— "Consonant blends are where it's at."

Administrative Style: Gets passionately involved in whatever is educationally relevant this month. She has been through behavior modification, ethnic studies, multicultural awareness, and right brain/left brain. When the top brain/bottom brain experts come around, she will be there. She is a survivor.

Proudest Accomplishment: In 1976, she threatened to quit unless the Board of Education approved an emergency appropriation for 1,200 copies of *Trout Fishing in America*, a very relevant book at the time.

Favorite Expression: From Heraclitus—"There is nothing permanent except change."

Prize Possession: The manuscript of her memoirs: *Taking the Right Turn: One Woman's Journey from Democratic Facilitator to Accountable Manager.*

Mr. Warden

Background: The word is he fulfilled his administrative internship by performing search-and-destroy missions with the Green Berets.

Educational Philosophy: "Under our Constitution every student has the right to a speedy sentence."

Administrative Style: Sweeps the campus regularly in an effort to suspend tokers, smokers, and class-cutters. Students in need of a two-day vacation have learned how to be in the wrong place at the right time.

Proudest Accomplishment: Enforcing with evenhanded ruthlessness his "No Hats Rule"—the regulation that has made of Lambert High School a millinery wasteland. In introducing the "No Hats Rule," he explained its purpose: "You shouldn't wear hats because I say you shouldn't wear hats."

Favorite Expression: "What are you trying to get away with?"

Prize Possession: A copy of *The Wit and Wisdom of John Wayne*, autographed by the Duke himself.

Mr. Optimist

Background: Raised in a home where Christian love was tempered with a "good stroppin'" when he misbehaved.

Educational Philosophy: "We've got to help these kids set high goals." There is no child who can't be saved if we're willing to give that child a few encouraging words and a few whacks across the butt.

Administrative Style: Pushes for "visible" programs that improve "self-concept." Is forever trying to get the newspapers and local TV station to pick up stories about "his kids." Right now he's working with a local hospital to make some of his reluctant readers "Brain Surgeons for a Day." He's just waiting for the go-ahead from Lloyd's of London.

Proudest Accomplishment: The day students in his school "just happened" to show up at polling booths where a school tax levy was being voted on and sang a few choruses of "The Lord Jesus Loves a Generous Citizen" as the TV cameras rolled. (The tax levy "just happened" to pass.)

Favorite Expression: "This spanking is going to hurt me a lot more than it's going to hurt you." (And he's not kidding, either.)

Prize Possession: His mama's sweet-potato pie, which, when it turns up at faculty pot lucks, is guaranteed to make his teachers forgive him for all the times he pulled students out of their classes in order to have them go sing at polling booths.

Mr. Bearingball

Background: Began as a P.E. teacher/football coach. Developed a teacher constituency while moonlighting as a life-insurance salesman specializing in an educator clientele.

Educational Philosophy: "You can't get a hit if you don't swing the bat. I like teachers and kids who'll take a good cut at the ball."

Administrative Style: Encourages the faculty to get to the games—where he makes a little list of those teachers who are not there supporting the team. When Middleberg High wins, he destroys his list, silently declaring a general amnesty to commemorate the victory. When Middleberg High loses, he destroys his list, relieved that more people were not present to witness the debacle.

Proudest Accomplishment: In the face of a hostile faculty, this principal approved the star quarterback for varsity play even though the boy had an F in chemistry. "The kid stood in there swinging," he said.

Favorite Expression: "What's the good word today?" Mr. Bearingball does not like to leave a lot of room open for bitching and moaning.

Prize Possession: His beefcake frame, a reminder of his glory days on the playing field. "Lose it, and I'd look like some damned ex-English teacher," he tells his drinking buddies.

Mr. Gladhand

Background: As former director of the Updale Union High School Band, he made his reputation leading his aggregation to shopping-mall openings. Even now he'll get into uniform and take his musicians out to perform at the anniversary celebration of any chocolate-chip-cookie store that has bought an ad in the school newspaper. "Community involvement," he calls it.

Educational Philosophy: "They come in here bellyaching about $6,000 worth of library books stolen last year. But hey, those kids are reading! I mean, THOSE KIDS ARE READING!"

Administrative Style: Moves about the building telling the Daily Joke, delivered to him each morning by the junior varsity basketball coach—who knows a lot of bartenders.

Proudest Accomplishment: Having Updale High picked as one of the five American high schools visited by educational representatives from the People's Republic of China, an honor somewhat tarnished when the Chinese envoys failed to appreciate the one about the foot-long penis on the railroad track.

Favorite Expression: "Why so glum, chum? Hey, did you hear the one about..."

Prize Possession: The copy of *Jokes for the John* his secretary gave him last Christmas.

The Principal at Work

Many teachers are confused about exactly what it is that principals do. Here, through a sampling of administrative memos principals have written, is documentation of this official's function.

The Principal Communicates with Key Parents

> To: Ms. Jane Balderdash,
>   P.T.A. President, Kingsbury Elementary School
> Jane—
> The cafeteria manager and I have discussed your plan for alternative food service, and while we agree that the children would certainly feel comfortable with the concept of P.T.A. officers and other mommies serving peanut-butter-and-jelly sandwiches and ice-cold milk at the noon meal, we believe that in the long run, our tuna-noodle casserole provides better preparation for life.

The Principal Implements School Board Policy

> To: The Faculty
> From: Your Principal
> In keeping with the national effort to develop a more rigorous curriculum, the School Board has selected Central High as the pilot school in which to offer a "beefed-up" academic program. The board is directing that, starting this fall, all Central students take five years of math, foreign language, English, and science. I have pointed out to the board that as Central High is a four-year institution, their "Five-in-Four Plan" presents certain logistical problems.
>
> However, they remind me that it is a considerable honor to be chosen as a pilot school, one on the cutting edge of educational reform, and that Central's fine faculty has met challenges before. So OK, geniuses. Tell me what to do now.

The Principal Relieves Faculty Paranoia

> To: All Faculty
> Several of you have asked that senior class vice-
> president Hershel Martinez be banned from bringing
> his tape recorder to your classes. He categorically
> denies he intends to produce, as has been rumored, a
> tape entitled "Great Bloopers and Boo-Boos from
> Andrew Jackson High." He says the senior class is
> planning other fund-raising activities. Let's give the kid
> the benefit of the doubt.

The Principal Calms Explosive Situations

> To: All Manatook High School Faculty and Students
> As you have probably heard by now, last Friday,
> before our football game with Hillsmont High, vandals
> carved "F——Manatook" in the 4-H Club's prizewinning
> zucchini plants. I want you to know that the culprits
> will be swiftly apprehended and punished. We are
> fortunate at Manatook to have a student body that does
> not feel the need to resort to this sort of childish act.
> Hillsmont is particularly lucky that none of its puny
> zucchini plants are big enough to cut up.

The Principal Solves Practical Problems, Creatively

> To: George Medroras, Print Shop Teacher
> Re: My latest bright idea
> George—
> You heard we've had a devil of a time getting parents
> to open mailers from the school? I wonder, can you get
> the kids to print, "You may already have won!" on the
> outside of each of these 50,000 envelopes? If we do this,
> I think we may get a better response.

The Principal Guides Teachers Toward Proper On-the-Job Conduct.

To: All Teachers
From: James McWorthy, Principal, Fall River High
I strongly advise that those of you who have taken to wearing buttons that read, "Lower the Thinking Age to 16," inform your students that you are taking an individual position that does not necessarily represent school-district policy.

The Principal Facilitates Teacher–Parent Communication

To: Fred Rauchman, Biology Teacher
Mr. Rauchman—
I have had a phone call from a Ms. Hamilton who claims that when her son Daniel asked if he could make up a test he missed due to absence, your response was, "Not really." Ms. Hamilton wonders if there is a difference between "Not really" and "No." Can you clarify this?

The Principal Arbitrates Spats Between Teachers and Support Personnel

To: All Faculty
The cafeteria manager, Mrs. Sloane, has called to my attention the fact that certain teachers are purchasing coffee at 8:00 A.M., then returning several hours later for a half-priced refill. Yesterday when a teacher became indignant after Mrs. Sloane refused him a refill $30\frac{1}{2}$ hours after his original purchase, she came to me. We need to find a solution to this problem, but I don't want to be arbitrary. I think the best way to go is a joint cafeteria-faculty refill committee. Any volunteers?

★★★

The Administrator's Pocket Guide to Teacher Hiring

★★★

Unbeknownst to teachers, administrators carry in their pockets a slim book called *Picking the Lesser of Many Evils: A Guide to Teacher Hiring*. Using easy-to-understand words and pictures, the book aids the administrator in selecting new faculty members. A copy of the book's contents appears below:

Beware this happy face. Anyone contemplating a teaching career who wears this kind of lobotomized smirk is either a doper, an airhead, or a Moonie.

Stay away from the guy with the bemused look, unless you want your every dangling modifier— supplemented by mean-spirited annotations— to make its way to the teachers' bulletin board.

Don't Do It. You may think this guy will be able to scare the kids into staying in their seats, but he can also scare you into a mild case of paranoia. You will not pass him in the hall without imagining some grievance he is getting ready to file over losing his duty-free prep period or some other inalienable rights.

Look Out. A crooked smile is a cynical smile. This guy will make his own rules. His students will likely never hear of the essay contest in conjunction with Ground Beef Week. He's the type who will treat a cheerleader just like any other kid—even on game day.

This Is It—the "Night of the Living Dead Look," as it's known in the trade—a study in perfect pliability. You have here your sock hop chaperon, your yearbook sponsor, and whatever else you need. A rare breed. *Snap him up.*

9

Teachers: The Myths, The Jokes

Some people on this planet come and go with nothing to show for it. Not teachers. We leave behind us a legacy of myths and jokes which our students make certain get passed on to subsequent generations. And so, while we may die, the tale of the morning we accidentally swallowed our contact lens will live. It is a kind of immortality...

The Great Teacher Myths

In recent years, Teacher Archetype Myths, transmitted by students, have been a hot item among anthropologists hard up for Ph.D. dissertation topics. These scholars note that certain school myths are confined to particular circumstances. For instance, it is only in schools that have three floors or a number of out-of-the-way nooks and crannies that the mythological tale of the Fossilized Classroom circulates. Here, the story is told, there

exists somewhere in the building a fossilized classroom, complete with fossilized students and a fossilized teacher. According to the legend, the last words to have issued from this site were, "No one is leaving this room until I get a right answer."

In general, however, scholars find that the same Teacher Archetype Myths circulate among students in every school:

The Teacher Who Doesn't Give A's.

Every student claims to have heard of the teacher who has given only one A in thirty-three years of teaching, and that to a certain Alvin Horowitz, now doing hard time at Sing Sing.

The Teacher Who Talks to Furniture.

Tales are told of the teacher who talks to the furniture, tales substantiated by students who have passed his room and heard, "Table Three, will you be quiet, Table Three."

134

The Teacher Who Gives "Surprise" Quizzes.

There is always talk of the teacher who has announced a surprise quiz every Friday for the last thirty years.

The Teacher Who Always Wears the Same Clothes.

Who doesn't know about the teacher who appears to have worn the same brown slacks and blue pin-striped jacket every day for the past fifteen years (but actually has at home five pairs of brown slacks and five blue pin-striped jackets which he rotates every school week).

The Teacher Who Smells.

Rumors fly about the teacher who ignores the seven or more "helpful hint" bottles of Scope presented by anonymous donors each Christmas.

The Teacher Who Likes Her Boys Big Where It Counts.

Chatter persists about the teacher who rewards with an A any boy with very large feet.

The Teacher Who is a Fascist at Heart.

Students prattle on about the teacher who seizes and locks in a cabinet any uncovered textbook and refuses to return it until it is covered.

The Teacher with a Past.

Everyone knows that one teacher camouflages his checkered history: once a dope dealer, then a monk, now a driver education teacher.

The Teacher with Lust in His Heart.

One source of endless gossip is the teacher who observes his cardinal educational principle: the shorter the skirt, the higher the grade.

The Spitting Teacher.

It's common knowledge that one teacher cannot cajole even the most eager students into sitting in the first two rows of his class, since they are unwilling to endure the saliva shower that accompanies his enthusiastic lectures.

The Drunken Teacher.

Hearsay reports circulate of the teacher who pulls the shade and locks the door of her room each noon, then scarfs the two shots of Old Crow and the egg-salad sandwich she'll need to get through the rest of the day.

The Easy Teacher.

The buzz seldom ceases about the teacher who hands out at the beginning of the school year a thirteen-page syllabus of "minimal expectations," but, in fact, gives an A to any student who copies seven pounds of notes from the *World Book Encyclopedia*.

The Teacher Who Cracked Up.

It's all over the school about the teacher, terrorized and reduced to tears by her third-period class, who has packed up and left the building, never to return. The odd thing is, she is always back for fifth period.

Teacher Jokes: The Classics

Right now your students are out there circulating totally tasteless teacher jokes of a sort we have no intention of writing about in this totally tasteful volume. Rather we present here some classics of the genre which, while they may have been considered vulgar at the time of their hazy origins, now have taken on a cozy antique charm. The categories established here may help you recall some old chestnuts of your own.

The Show-and-Tell Disaster

One day during show-and-tell period, the teacher asked the students to stand up and tell something interesting that had happened to them on the way to school.

When Mary's turn came, she got up and said, "On the way to school, I saw a flat dog."

"A flat dog?" asked the teacher, uncomprehending.

"Well, I think it was flat," said Mary, "cause another dog was behind it pumping it up."

The Confused Teacher

At the faculty Christmas party, Ms. Fillup, the English teacher, asked Mr. Friptop, the math teacher, "Will you pass the nuts?"

"I suppose so," said Mr. Friptop, "though personally I'd like to flunk every one of them."

The Confused Kid

A schoolteacher was trying to correct Johnny in class for using incorrect English.

Johnny said to his teacher, "I ain't got no pencil."

The teacher corrected him at once. "It's 'I don't have a pencil'; 'They don't have any pencils'; 'We don't have any pencils.' Is that clear?"

"No," said the bewildered Johnny. "What happened to all them pencils?"

The Kid with a Body

"Teacher," said Mary, "I have to go to the bathroom."

"All right, Mary," said the teacher, "but you know the rule: First you recite the alphabet."

Mary began: "A-B-C-D-E-F-G-H-I-J-K-L-M-N-O-Q-R-S-T-U-V-W-X-Y-Z."

"Very good, Mary, but what happened to the 'P'?" asked the teacher.

"Right now, the 'P' is running down my leg, Teacher," said Mary.

The Teacher with a Body

It was the first day of school, and the nervous teacher trying to make a good impression had a little gas in the stomach. When finally, matters reached the point where she could not control it, she did her best to release a little crunchy one. What she got instead was a veritable explosion. Desperate, she looked down at Johnny in the first row, "Johnny, you stop that," she said.

"If it comes my way, Teacher, I sure will try," said Johnny.

The Sexy Kid

A teacher was having trouble with her class. She decided to do something to gain the class's attention, so she came to school in a pair of tight pants. Shortly after class began, she said, "Now, it's time for a riddle. I have something in my right pocket that is round and orange and soft. Who can tell what kind of fruit it is?"

Johnny, one of the instigators of the trouble, raised his hand and said, "I know. It's an orange."

"No, Johnny, it is a peach. But that shows that you're thinking."

Later she gave the same description of the fruit in her other pocket, and Johnny guessed again—this time "peach."

"No, Johnny," replied the teacher, "It's an orange, but that shows you're thinking."

As class ended, Johnny raised his hand and said, "Teacher, I have in my pocket something that I'm holding on to that is long and hard and has a red tip on the end."

"Johnny, you stay after school!" said the teacher.

"Why, Teacher?" said Johnny. "I was only talking about my pencil. But that shows you're thinking."

The Sexy Teacher

One day the teacher stood on her toes to write on the blackboard, and one of the boys in the class giggled.

TEACHER: Johnny, what is the matter?

JOHNNY: Oh, Teacher, I saw your slip.

TEACHER: Well, for that I am going to send you home for two days.

And Johnny went home for two days. When he came back, the teacher leaned over to erase the blackboard, and he giggled again.

TEACHER: Johnny, what is the matter this time?

JOHNNY: Oh, Teacher, I saw your garters.

TEACHER: Well, for that, I am going to send you home for a week.

And Johnny went home for a week. When he came back, the teacher bent over to pick up some chalk. She heard Johnny giggle, and she turned around to see him walking out of the room.

TEACHER: And where are you going?

JOHNNY: Teacher, my school days are over.

The Rebellious Kid

Mary, her teacher noticed, was always peering into her cupped hands. One day, the teacher asked, "Mary, what have you got in your hands?"

"Shit," said Mary.

The teacher, appalled but containing himself, then asked, "And what are you doing with it, Mary?"

"Makin' a teacher," Mary said.

Well, this was just too much, so he sent Mary to the principal. The principal was a little angry, but nice, and she asked, "Mary, what have you got in your hands?"

And Mary answered, "Shit."

"And what are you *doing* with it, Mary?"

"Makin' a principal."

Well, the principal decided that this kid needed *help*, so she sent Mary to the school guidance counselor. The counselor sat Mary down, and said very sweetly, "Now, Mary, what have you got in your hands?"

"Shit," Mary answered innocently.

The counselor, very friendly but now just a bit condescending, said, "Oh, Mary, and now I suppose you're going to tell me that you're making a guidance counselor."

"Nope," said Mary. "Not enough shit."

🍎10🍎
Those Who Can...
Teach

The Road Not Taken

Sometimes (usually no more than three times an hour), you think about leaving teaching. But you're nervous. Sure, you can alphabetize your roll book in one-half preparation period flat. Of course, you can negotiate with Charlie's Chuckwagon for a $10.95 dinner (tax and gratuity included) honoring the supply clerk's retirement. Yet deep down, you wonder if you really have the smarts to manage a Pizza Hut. The answer is, "Of course you do." The World of Business Opportunity is slavering for people with the very skills you have learned staying more or less alive at Hacksome High School. Right now you could be the successful owner of:

A telephone answering service. Just recall how the classroom phone always rings for Tina Morello, who is wanted in the Dean's Office right away, or for Mr. MacCallum, who has the room four doors down, and you will realize you are a natural for this business.

A collection agency. You were the one who spotted Sheri Silverman's

general math book, missing for four months, in the dumpster in front of the girls' gym. You managed to unearth Robbie Grinell's father after two and a half years and a court order. You'll have no trouble at all repossessing Oldsmobiles in the dead of night.

Escort service. You looked the other way when the French teacher played *cherchez la femme* with anyone impressionable, nubile, and sixteen. As class sponsor, you pretended the purpose of the senior picnic was to have a picnic. It's time you made some money off your tolerance of hanky-panky.

Travel agency. Sure, any travel bureau can send clients off to London, Paris, and Rome, but how many of them would have the geographical imagination to arrange a grand tour of landlocked countries or one of the major flax-exporting nations of the world?

A restaurant. Try a theme restaurant—maybe "School Daze." Sell free lunch passes to patrons as they enter. Hire middle-aged women, wearing hairnets and Space shoes, to work behind a steam table

139

serving things made of macaroni. Arrange for the maitre d' to assign detention to those customers who do not bus their dishes.

A translation service. For years you have been working with those curriculum specialists who want you to "strategize" and "replicate." You have, at least, pretended you can make English of their densest prose. Translating Serbo-Croatian should be easy.

A nightclub. At the average nightclub, a bunch of people wearing fashionably bizarre clothes show up to see and be seen and to negotiate deals for drugs and sex while ostensibly there to dance. Substitute "learn" for "dance" in the above sentence and you will see where your experience fits in.

A driving school. If you have been able to keep your cool while generations of students mislabel gerunds, butcher *passé composé*, and blank out on geometry proofs, you certainly have the patience to tolerate the klutziest efforts at parallel parking.

A cult. To be a cult leader, you need to be able to convince your followers that you are not quite human, that what seems important is absurd and what seems absurd is important, and that they will Lose Points if they screw up. Doesn't that sound pretty much like what you do every third period?

As You Near Retirement...

Time has a way... One day you're telling a class for the first time, "My name is Miss Blanchard," and then, 3,800 Daily Attendance Reports later, you're packing up your desk copy of *Roget's Thesaurus* for the last time. So what's changed over those years? Here's a little inventory.

★★

Then	**Now**
You had five classes of remedial students who could not properly understand McGruder's *American Government*.	You have five classes of advanced students who cannot properly understand McGruder's *American Government*.
★ ★ ★	
Kids who screwed up were called "maladjusted."	Kids who screw up are called "gifted."
★ ★ ★	

★★

If you didn't lead the flag salute, you were in big trouble.

What flag?

* * *

The New Grammar and the New Math came along to make these confusing subjects less difficult.

The Old Confusions have been reinstated.

* * *

Curriculum Assistants had little cubbyhole offices where they developed units on forest conservation.

Little cubbyholes are now inhabited by equally useful computers.

* * *

A student caught reading *Fanny Hill* in class would be in big trouble.

A student caught reading anything in class may be on his way to a National Merit Scholarship.

* * *

You were assigned a windowless classroom next to the beginning band room.

You have acquired a choice room with a view of a street regularly assaulted by jackhammers.

* * *

Surprise fire drills occurred in the middle of tests.

Fire drills still occur in the middle of tests, but nothing surprises you anymore.

* * *

You were required to use a pay phone in the basement for personal calls.

You are allowed to make personal calls from a school phone while two clerks and an office monitor eavesdrop.

* * *

Students were meticulously tracked into "high normal," "average normal," and "low normal" groups.

No one is normal.

★ ★ ★

You were reprimanded by your vice-principal because your classroom windows were not open four inches from the top.

With the boards that have replaced the broken windows, opening the windows is no problem.

★ ★ ★

You reprimanded your students by saying, "School is not a social club."

Now you are not so sure.

★ ★ ★

Little squabbles broke out among students contesting for the privilege of carrying your books.

It is a major test of your charisma to recruit an eraser monitor.

★ ★ ★

There were special enrichment programs for culturally deprived kids.

With the advent of MTV, either all the kids or none of the kids are culturally deprived, depending on how you look at it.

The Student Reporter Asks:

As an extremely old and wise person, and one who keeps telling us every year that you are going to retire, if you actually do retire before you die or something like that, what would you do to commemorate your retirement? Please be specific.

"What I'd do is go back through the old yearbooks and make up a slide show of memorable students from the past, those that dared to be different. There was the kid who would come into class every day with a little problem for me, such as, "Tell me six ways to avoid stepping on ants," or the boy who set out to memorize the dictionary and actually made it as far as "bouil-labaisse," or the girl who could draw by memory, down to the smallest detail, any fighter plane of World War II. I would show these slides at my retirement dinner and I would narrate the show in a tone that would suggest the viewers were being treated to a glimpse of some rare and exotic treasure, as indeed they would be. They would be looking at people who, by age seventeen, had decided they would be themselves."

—An older teacher

Dear Teacher,

Somebody told us you might not be ~~here~~ hear next year. Please say ~~its~~ ~~its~~ not so because we need you. You are the Kind of person who ~~actually gives a shit about Kids.~~ is nice. So get lots of rest this summer because you will need it when you meet us. Ha ha!

Sincerely,
Your students next year